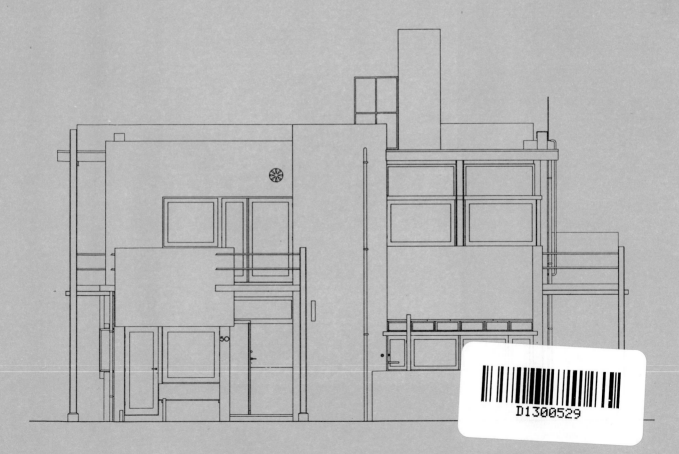

50

The Rietveld Schröder House

# The Rietveld Schröder House

Paul Overy
Lenneke Büller
Frank den Oudsten
Bertus Mulder

First English edition

© 1988 The Massachusetts Institute of
Technology

© 1988 Vorm + Kleur, Naarden

Library of Congress Cataloging-in-
Publication Data

Overy, Paul, 1940
The Rietveld Schröder House.

Includes bibliographical references and
index.
1. Rietveld, Gerrit Thomas, 1888-1964
    — Criticism and interpretation
2. Schröder Huis (Utrecht, Netherlands)
3. Architecture, Modern — 20th century
    — Netherlands — Utrecht.
4. Utrecht (Netherlands) — Buildings,
    structures, etc.
5. Schröder, Truus, 1889-1985 — Homes
    and haunts — Netherlands — Utrecht.
6. Modernism (Art) — Influence.
7. De Stijl (Art movement) — Influence.
    I. Title.
8. Büller, Lenneke; Oudsten, Frank den
9. Mulder, Bertus

NA.1153.R5.094 1988
728.3'72'0924
87-36176
ISBN 0-262-15033-6

Printed in Spain

# Contents

Dust cover: first floor, 1987, view of the stairwell/landing and the
living-dining area. In the foreground the Red Blue chair
Cover inset: Southwest facade. Drawing by Han Schröder, 1951

Dust cover, inside left: southeast facade
Dust cover, inside right: northeast facade
Drawings by Han Schröder, 1951

Facing the title page: Rietveld; axonometric drawing of the first
floor, undated

# Foreword

People react slowly, and this applies to architecture too. Usually we only discover the significance of a building after we have grown completely accustomed to it. The passage of time plays an important role here. The shock of the first impact slowly ebbs, and after many years we appreciate what an enormous effect it must have had when it was first built. This is what happened with the Rietveld Schröder House. In 1924 the public beheld an unusual phenomenon and reacted critically, while even those familiar with modern architectural ideas were surprised, and discussed it cautiously.

Slowly but surely it became an established part of Prins Hendriklaan and people grew accustomed to it; it became a frequent topic in professional literature. But despite this, it was many years after the Second World War before people realized just how important this house was in the development of 'modern architecture', both conceptually and formally.

It seems as if we could only come to terms with this comparatively early work by Rietveld once the criticism of functionalism had led to a reassessment of autonomous design. And as a result, Rietveld's later work — the majority of his oeuvre — has been pushed into the background. We should ask whether this does not do Rietveld a great injustice.

In this first house we find the blueprint for all Rietveld's later ideas about domestic architecture and ways of living in it. In view of this the cooperation with his commissioner, Truus Schröder-Schräder, receives a particular emphasis. The assignment that she presented undoubtedly had a stimulating effect on Rietveld's search for more generally valid solutions to problems about flexible use of space, the relationship between a building and its surroundings and the provision of facilities in the home. These were elements that for Truus Schröder constituted a new outlook on society.

It almost goes without saying that when the significance of the house was rediscovered, restoration work was begun; the Rietveld Schröder House Foundation regarded the restoration of the house as a stimulating necessity. The house has now been opened to the public, under the motherly supervision of the Central Museum in Utrecht, so that many people can now experience the results of an exciting metamorphosis of space in this highly personal and unique building.

In his introductory essay, Paul Overy discusses the origins and history of the house, and provides a lively picture of the building itself and its occupant. To give further insight into this work of Rietveld, he discusses some of his early furniture in relation to the design of the house. The description he gives is one that could only be provided by someone who had observed long, carefully, and intimately.

Over a period of several years, Lenneke Büller and Frank den Oudsten have been deeply involved with the Rietveld Schröder House. Their knowledge of architecture and in particular the major works of the 1920s, led them to study this building in great detail. A few years ago they made a number of documentary works about De Stijl, the Schröder house and its occupant, Mrs Schröder.

The interview with Mrs Schröder published here was recorded in 1982. Furthermore, Frank den Oudsten made two detailed photographic reports of the house; the first in 1981 for the exhibition *De Stijl 1917-1931, Visions of Utopia*, the second in spring 1987, shortly after completion of the restoration. Their contribution to this book is based on this unique material, and greatly adds to our understanding of the house and the ideas that inspired it.

The painstaking restoration of the house was assigned to the architect Bertus Mulder. His former collaboration with Rietveld, and his long involvement in the upkeep of the house, made him the perfect candidate for this task. To do this, he analyzed the way the house had been constructed, discounting the myths which had accumulated around it, with a pragmatic approach that matched that of Rietveld. It is from this particular point of view that Mulder describes the house and its restoration.

In this restoration, no attempt has been made to reproduce the house exactly as it was in 1924-1925; the house is now a concentration of the essence of what Rietveld and Mrs Schröder intended it to be. We thought this would be the most accurate way of presenting the original vision of Truus Schröder-Schräder and Gerrit Rietveld. This book provides valuable background information.


Wim Crouwel

*Chairman of the Rietveld Schröder House Foundation*
*Director of the Boymans-van Beuningen Museum, Rotterdam*

Above: plan of the first floor, showing sliding partitions opened
Drawing by Bertus Mulder, 1987
Below: first floor, 1987; sliding partitions opened, with view of Mrs
Schröder's bedroom, the stairwell/landing and living-dining area

Above: plan of the first floor, showing sliding partitions closed
Drawing by Bertus Mulder, 1987
Below: same view as page 10; sliding partitions partly closed, and
the movable window on the staircase railings in the position so that
the living-dining area and stairwell/landing are seperated from
each other

PAUL OVERY

# Introduction

The Rietveld Schröder House has probably been more reproduced and more influential than any other domestic building of the early modern period, including the villas of Le Corbusier. Certainly it has had a more direct effect on people's lives. For it was the first open-plan house, a prototype of how many live today who have never heard of this small semi-detached house in Utrecht and who would still find its forthright 'modernity' alarming. Built more than sixty years ago the house has recently been restored to something close to its original condition. How is it possible to view such an icon of modernism in a period when the general public and many architects have rejected the principles of modernism?

But modernism is not a unitary concept; it has many meanings which are constantly shifting and evolving. The architectural modernism which has been so decisively rejected in recent years was a creation of the 1950s and 1960s — bearing only a distant relationship to the early modernist architecture of the inter-war period — manifested at its crudest and most socially destructive in the large-scale tower, slab or deck-access blocks employed almost universally for mass working class housing until the late 1970s. Like many of the most original designs of the early modernist period the Schröder house played only a peripheral part in the construction of post-war modernism, even though its originality was recognised and given iconic status. For what the Schröder house represented — the intimate domestic scale, the flexible open plan of the first floor which could be either open or closed according to the needs or wishes of the occupants, the employment of colour and form to create a space related to human dimensions and living requirements — was conspicuously elided from modernist architectural practice in the 1960s and early 1970s.

When the Schröder house was first built it did not connote 'modernism' so much as 'modernity'. (Modernism, as opposed to modernity, only began to emerge as a concept in the early 1930s.) Yet that modernity — the modernity of the 1920s — is something very different from any current understanding of the term. Then modernity construed difference; today similarity. Then to be in the 'avant-garde', today conformism. We are post-modern only in that we can now see the 'modern' period as historical, one of the many periods of the past which may be plundered for their stylistic forms and surfaces, parodied or pastiched. The modernity we have to live with today is drained of the idealism and fantasy of the early modernism represented by icons of the modern movement like the Schröder house. Part of their function as 'monuments', as texts of modernism, is to re-inscribe that fantasy and idealism, to map out territory which has been lost and which, by means of history and myth, can be repossessed, made usable again.

The passage of time has changed these buildings, irrevocably altered their relationship to the fabric of living which has moved on around them. Restoring a building like the Schröder house to a close approximation of how it *looked* sixty years ago does not, of course, turn the clock back. But it does, however, alter the sedimented layers of shifting meanings accumu-

Ground floor, 1987
Left: the study with the 1925 Armchair
Above: the study, looking towards the ceiling. The ceiling of the hall
beside it is also visible, through the window strip

lated with the passing of time. The Schröder house has been made to visually resemble a house newly built sixty years ago; yet those sixty years of history cannot be so easily expunged. Meanings cannot be stripped off or overlaid like coats of paint; although changed, they remain, affecting subsequent meanings.

When the house was built it was the last house in the city. It was also, in another sense, the first. It was 'on the edge' both literally and metaphorically. Now it is neither the first nor the last; its new status is ambiguous. Where the house once looked onto open countryside, it now faces a raised motorway along which cars and lorries rush past at the level of the first floor living area with its wide windows designed to give an uninterrupted view of meadows and fields. The modernity which the house once seemed so fiercely to convey is now more clearly inscribed in the crude concrete of the orbital motorway or the vast shopping centre and transport complex Hoog Catharijne which dominates the centre of present day Utrecht.

In the face of such monolithic modernity, the Schröder house looks touchingly fragile and temporary. The modernity which it represents is not the modernity of today, but a way of life conceived and lived out in the early decades of the 20th century. Mrs Schröder, who commissioned the house in 1924, continued to live in it until her death in 1985 at the age of 95. Her longevity created an unusual continuity between the past and the present. This should not conceal the fact that the house had already in her lifetime become a monument of early modernism.

It is difficult perhaps to see such a small and unprepossessing building as a 'monument'. In reality it looks even smaller than it appears in photographs. One is constantly surprised *how* small and unluxurious the Schröder house is. This is emphasised by the awkward way it is attached to the large ungainly block of early 20th century brick-built apartment houses next door. When it was new the house turned towards the open countryside at the edge of the city, away from these houses which represented the traditional, 'comfortable' bourgeois values that it was designed to deny. Since its restoration and opening to the public the house is now connected by a door knocked through the wall of the next building, the ground floor of which has become a study centre and display space. Although this cannot be perceived from the outside, it may be taken to signify that the Schröder house has finally been absorbed into tradition, into history. Its historical position depends on its reception during the intervening years and the life led in it by its 'patroness, inspirer, and joint-inventor' [1] Mrs Schröder. For her contribution was not completed by the initiation and co-design of the house with the architect Gerrit Rietveld. Until the end of her life Mrs Schröder continued to play out the role she had created for herself in relation to the house. By continuing to live there for sixty years, she demonstrated by her example how modern architecture might be lived in. And increasingly in later years she was able to control and construct the position she wanted the house to occupy in history by means of the promotion and documentation of

1. Peter Smithson, June 1979, in Alison and Peter Smithson, *The Heroic Period of Modern Architecture,* London 1981, p.19

2. The flexibility of the interior with its sliding screens and the built-in furniture were Mrs Schröder's major contributions to the design.

its historical and iconic status in the development of 20th century architecture and design.

The house was essentially a dialogue: the result of an exceptional architect-client relationship. Rietveld and Mrs Schröder designed much of the equipment and built-in furniture for the house together. [2] During the next few years after the house was completed Mrs Schröder and Rietveld collaborated on a number of architectural projects and furniture designs and Rietveld kept a studio and a space to work in the house until 1932. [3] Much later, after his wife died in 1958, Rietveld came to live in the house for the last six years of his life. In the six decades after it was completed the house underwent a number of minor alterations. Most of these were made by Mrs Schröder and Rietveld in collaboration until his death in 1964.

To visit the house in Mrs Schröder's lifetime was an extraordinary experience. This was a house in which a family had grown up and which had responded organically to their changing needs and to those of Mrs Schröder herself. Today this layering of experience, of lives lived in the house, only survives in photographs. Before her death Mrs Schröder made the house over to the foundation which would donate it to the municipality as a museum and study-centre. [4] She also arranged with the foundation and the architect Bertus Mulder (who had worked for Rietveld) that the house should be restored so that the interior space would be as close as possible to its original state. This was done in 1986-87 on the basis of photographs taken shortly after the house was completed, the memories of her three children, and numerous discussions between Mulder and Mrs Schröder before her death. The restored house was opened in April 1987.

However it is not possible to visit the Schröder house as it was when it was first completed. [5] We are in the final decades of the 20th century, not the first. The restored house is a brilliant reconstruction, a careful historical re-creation. But, although visually it bears an almost exact resemblance to it, this is not the house which the thirty-five-year-old Mrs Schröder moved into in December 1924 as a widow with three small children. It is a house with over six decades of private and public history.

The fame of the house spread remarkably quickly. Its initial renown was largely due to the ceaseless propagandizing activities of the artist, designer, writer and propagandist, Theo van Doesburg, who published photographs and descriptions of the house in the *De Stijl* magazine which he edited, and constantly brought it to the attention of the international avant-garde of the 1920s. [6] Van Doesburg died in 1931 and the house received less attention in the changing intellectual, economic and political climate of the 1930s. But after the second world war, when modernist architecture won world-wide acceptance in the 1950s and 1960s, the reputation of the Schröder house was securely established.

3. Between 1924 and 1938, Rietveld and Mrs Schröder worked together on the following projects:
Rietveld Schröder House, 1924
Glass radio cabinet, 1925
Hanging glass cabinet, 1926
Project for standardized housing, 1927
Interior Birza house, Amsterdam, 1927
Van Urk house, Blaricum, 1930-31
Desk, 1931
Houses on Erasmuslaan, Utrecht, 1930-34
Vreeburg Cinema, Utrecht, 1936
Movable summer houses, 1936
Interiors 'Ekawo', Haarlem, 1938
The apartment block opposite the Schröder House, in Erasmuslaan, was erected by Rietveld and Mrs Schröder as a speculative venture, for it had become clear that the open country across which the Schröder house had originally faced was shortly going to be built upon. Mrs Schröder wished to control what was put up opposite the house. In 1936 she lived in one of these apartments while alterations were being made to the Schröder House.

4. The Rietveld Schröder House Foundation was set up in 1970. The house became the property of the foundation and essential restoration work was carried out in 1974. In 1983 the house was handed over to the City of Utrecht on a long lease; this was made possible through the Utrecht Insurance Company AMEV. Since the Rietveld Schröder House opened to the public in 1987, the Central Museum, Utrecht has been responsible for its running and management.

5. The house was designed during the first few months of 1924. The drawing for the application for a building permit is dated 2 July; the contractor's estimate is dated 7 July; the building contract was signed on 9 July 1924. Probably the building as such was ready in October of that year. Mrs Schröder and her three children moved in at the end of 1924, while work was still being carried out on the interior and the furniture. The colour design of the interior was not completed until the summer of 1925. (Theodore Brown, *The work of G. Rietveld Architect,* Utrecht 1958, p. 155, note 27)

6. The De Stijl group of artists, architects and designers was founded by Theo van Doesburg in 1917. At various times during its existence (1917-31) its members included the artists Piet Mondrian, Bart van der Leck, Vilmos Huszár and Georges Vantongerloo, the architects J.J.P. Oud, Robert van 't Hoff, Jan Wils and Cornelis van Eesteren. Rietveld became a member of the group in 1919, Mrs. Schröder in 1925. The Schröder house was first published in De Stijl, Vol.6, No. 10-11, 1924-25, p. 160 (exterior) and Vol.6, No. 12, 1924-25, p. 140 (interior)

First floor, c.1925; view of the living-dining area with Mrs Schröder and her daughter Han, seated on the Berlin chair. Other furniture designs, from l. to r.: Military table, 1923, End table, 1923, Easy chair, 1924, Table lamp, 1925

Although he never received the monolithic status accorded to modernist architects like Le Corbusier, Gropius and Mies van der Rohe, in his later years Rietveld gained international recognition as an architect and designer, based on the reputation of the Schröder house and his early furniture designs. A major De Stijl retrospective was held in Amsterdam at the Stedelijk Museum in 1951. Rietveld's early work was strongly represented and he was responsible for the design of the exhibition which was also shown at the Museum of Modern Art, New York. During the last six years of Rietveld's life, when he was living in the Schröder house (1958-64), it was visited by many young architects, critics and architectural historians. After Rietveld's death, Mrs Schröder continued to welcome visitors encouraging architects, architectural and design historians, critics and photographers who would help to construct a historical role for the house. During the twenty years in which she survived Rietveld Mrs Schröder vigorously promoted his reputation and that of the Schröder house. And in reminiscences, interviews, letters and conversations she was also able to reconstruct her own part in its conception and design.

In some of the earliest published illustrations and descriptions of the house she and Rietveld are credited as joint designers.[7] Later when Rietveld became well-known as an architect this was often suppressed or forgotten. Today it is possible to re-establish and re-interpret Mrs Schröder's role in the conception and design of the house. This can now be clarified in the light of her own efforts to reconstruct its history, the re-assessments of critics and historians who have examined the house in new and more rigorous ways, and by recent attempts to reconstruct the role of women as patrons, collaborators and co-designers in the early history of the modern movement. The interview with Mrs Schröder recorded in 1982 and published here for the first time helps to make clear her own view of the collaborative process which went into the design of this small but extraordinary building. The careful and sympathetic restoration of the interior and its built-in furniture and equipment in 1986-87 has helped to re-establish Mrs Schröder's contribution to the design. For it was these elements which were most altered over the years, after her children had grown up and left home, and when different parts of the house were occupied by people who were not members of her family.[8]

When Mrs Schröder asked Rietveld to work on the Schröder house he had never designed a complete building before. His practice had been mainly as a furniture-maker, although three years previously in 1921 he had re-modelled Mrs Schröder's study in the 19th century house in which she lived with her husband and three young children at 135 Biltstraat, Utrecht. Mrs Schröder had no training or experience as a designer or architect, but she had a clear vision of how she wanted to live her life and the surroundings in which she wished to live it. She saw this as a demonstration of how living in the 20th century might be different from the 19th century life-styles which had persisted into the 1920s among people of all classes in Holland as elsewhere in Western Europe. Although her desire to live a new

7. For example *De Stijl*, Vol.6, No.10-11, 1924-25, p.160, where it is described as designed by 'G.Rietveld & Schräder'; and J.Badovici, 'Entretiens sur l'architecture vivante', in *L'Architecture Vivante*, Vol.5, Autumn and Winter, 1925 where the photograph of the house is captioned: 'Maison à Utrecht (Pays-Bas) par T.Schräder et G.Rietveld.' Schräder was Mrs Schröder's maiden name.

8. Some of the downstairs rooms were let out during the war and after Rietveld's death.

kind of life was conceived in terms of her own particular personal situation and social class, she seems to have believed that the house and the life that she lived in it might be the model for others.

———

Truus Schröder-Schräder was born in 1889 in Deventer in the east of Holland where her father owned a textile factory. Her mother died when she was four and her father remarried two years later. The family moved first to Leiden, then to Arnhem. Truus Schräder did not get on with her stepmother and was sent to a convent boarding school at Amersfoort. (Her family were Catholic.)

After leaving school she trained as a pharmacist and when she was twenty she went to live for some months with a Catholic family in England. In 1911 she married a lawyer F.A.C. Schröder who was eleven years older than her but from a similar prosperous Catholic background. (His family owned a factory in Brabant.) The Schröders had three children, a boy and two girls; they lived in a spacious apartment in Utrecht on the first floor of the large building in Biltstraat where Mr Schröder had his offices. This seems to have given Mrs Schröder a liking for living on the first floor which is one of the most striking features of the Schröder house. [9] She recalled that although she liked living in the apartment in Biltstraat she found the rooms too high and her husband suggested that she have one of them altered. [10] She describes her dissatisfaction with the house as a symptom of her discontent with the bourgeois life-style that she shared with her husband. The redesigning of the interior was a way of restructuring the life that could be led within the interior. This was the principle which guided her in the brief that she worked out with Rietveld when they began to plan the Schröder house. [11]

The room in the Biltstraat had been remodelled by building in seats and sofa beds, and by making the ceiling appear lower by covering the top parts of the tall windows, painting different parts of the walls in light greys and by replacing the lighting, notably with an arrangement of bare light bulbs hanging from the ceiling. This was similar to light fittings Rietveld had designed earlier for the G. & Z.C. jewelers shop in Kalverstraat, in Amsterdam. (It was seeing the maquette for this shop that had determined Mrs Schröder to ask Rietveld to redesign her room in the Biltstraat. [12]) She recalled that the family were shocked by the alterations because instead of revealing, however discreetly, that the Schröders were well-off professional people, the bareness and simplicity of the room seemed to deny this. [13] The room showed little trace of the luxury which such a family would unostentatiously but unmistakeably incorporate into their interiors, as into their own life style. But Mrs Schröder was concerned with establishing other criteria for living. For the people who came to admire her remodelled room were avant-garde architects like Bruno Taut and artists like Kurt Schwitters, not the jewelers and business people who were her husband's clients.

9. It was traditional among the Dutch mercantile classes to have their main living rooms on the first floor above their shops or business premises.

10. In the interview with Lenneke Büller and Frank den Oudsten, May, 1982, p.44

11. The German architect G.A.Platz described the Schröder house in 1933 as 'the best example of the "liberated dwelling". Here the emotional life of our era is convincingly expressed for the first time.' (G.A.Platz, *Wohnräume der Gegenwart,* Berlin 1933, p.39; quoted in Brown, 1958, p.59, original German p.156, note 49, op.cit.)

12. See interview, p.44. The shop was that of the Goldsmiths and Silversmiths Company. For a full description of the alterations made by Rietveld to Mrs Schröder's room in Biltstraat, see Bertus Mulder's article in *Rietveld Schröder Huis 1925-1975,* Utrecht 1975, p.22

13. See interview, pp.44,46

14. The Schröders belonged to the local art associations in Utrecht such as Kunstliefde (Love of Art) and Voor de Kunst (For Art). Mr Schröder was a member of Kunstliefde from 1913-16 and both he and Mrs Schröder were members of Voor de Kunst from 1918. (Marijke Küper, 'Gerrit Rietveld' in Carel Blotkamp (et. al.) *De Stijl: The Formative Years 1917-1922,* Cambridge, Massachusetts and London 1986, p.261; p.278.) Rietveld was also a member of Kunstliefde. He exhibited four paintings at the annual exhibition in 1912. Most of Rietveld's clients were professional people, many of whom belonged to these or similar associations. (See Küper, op.cit.)

15. This interior has been dismantled, but part of it is preserved in the collection of the Stedelijk Museum, Amsterdam.

16. The Schröder house was much smaller and built to a much cheaper specification than any of Le Corbusier's villas, or any other comparable domestic building of the early modern era. All the 'classic' modernist houses, by Le Corbusier, Adolf Loos, Mies van der Rohe, and other well-known architects of the period were very much more expensive and luxurious than the Schröder house. Its final cost ($f$ 11,000) was about the average for a small semi-detached house of the time in the Netherlands. (Brown, 1958, p.155, note 38, op.cit.)

17. The German critic, E.E.von Strasser wrote in 1926 that the Schröder house was 'the prototype of future housing.' (E.E.von Strasser, *Neuere holländische Baukunst*, Munich 1926, p.21; quoted in Brown, 1958, p.58, original German p.156, note 46, op.cit.) In 1941 Rietveld wrote: 'A cheap house (a so-called worker's house) must be a category of its own; it should not be a scaled-down middle-class house, just as this again is a scaled down version of a "gentlemen's house". As a result of mass production and industrialization, the product meant for the masses is no longer a replica or a reduced version of the product for the individual citizen, but rather a standard product. Thus the product intended for the individual is at best a luxury version of this basic form.' (*De 8 en Opbouw*, 1941, IX; quoted in *G.Rietveld Architect*, exhibition catalogue, Stedelijk Museum, Amsterdam 1971; Hayward Gallery, London 1972, np.) In the late 1920s and early 1930s Rietveld made designs for workers' houses (sometimes in collaboration with Mrs Schröder) but these were never carried out. In the late 1930s and early 1940s most of his commissions were villas for middle-class clients and he gained a reputation for being an 'exclusive' architect. Much later, towards the end of his life, Rietveld designed a working-class housing estate in Utrecht at Hoograven, in collaboration with Van Grunsven and H.Schröder (Mrs Schröder's youngest daughter)

Mrs Schröder's sister An Schräder was married to a surgeon R.J. Harrenstein. The Harrensteins lived in Amsterdam where they were part of a progressive circle frequented by artists. It is clear that Mrs Schröder wished to create a similar role for herself in Utrecht. [14] The design of the Schröder house can be seen as part of this project. (In 1926 Rietveld and Mrs Schröder completely remodelled the Harrenstein's Amsterdam apartment to create a light, bright space quite closely related to the interior of the Schröder house. [15]) When Mrs Schröder's husband died in 1923 at the age of 45, she was left to bring up three children aged between twelve and six on her own. Although she was adequately provided for it was necessary to leave the apartment in the Biltstraat and look for a smaller, cheaper and more convenient house. Her original idea was to ask Rietveld to remodel an existing building, but they could find nothing suitable and decided to build a new house. It was to be a very modest and inexpensive house. Perhaps it was because this was his first full architectural commission that Mrs Schröder was able to exert such a strong influence on its design. Trained as a craftsman Rietveld worked in a tradition which respected the requirements of the client in a quite different way from the professional architect. Significantly there was no formal commission of the kind usual between client and architect, only a contract with the builder.

Now that the interior of the Schröder house has been restored it is possible to see how plain and unluxurious it must have appeared. [16] However for the contemporary photographs on which the restoration was based, the minor disorders and messes of living were no doubt tidied away, so that the house appears in these as rather more severe and bare than it probably was in reality. (It was, after all, occupied by three children, according to whom Mrs Schröder was not a strict mother.) In later years Mrs Schröder added a greater degree of apparent comfort — although not of luxury — to the house. But it must have appeared to visitors, to neighbours, and to her late husband's family, as a house that rigorously avoided not only ostentation, but any attempt to inscribe in its fabric the traditional values of the prosperous Dutch middle classes. This must have appeared startling and shocking at the time; and it is clear that Truus Schröder-Schräder was a woman of extremely determined character who took a delight in provoking her more conventional contemporaries. The house was a statement of intent, a stance taken; a declaration of how an independent modern woman intended to live her life. It would be wrong, however, to see the Schröder house as in any way a prototype, or model for working class mass housing — despite its economic specification. It is far too individualistic. Rather it was a prototype for the 'reduced' circumstances of middle class living in the later part of the 20th century, when servants can no longer be afforded and space is at a premium. [17]

Although the Schröder house was constantly visited by artists and architects, it was not designed on the principle of the artist's studio like Le Corbusier's villas, and Mrs Schröder did not extensively collect works of art. [18] Rather the life lived in the house was to be a work of art in itself. It was to be the setting for a continuing celebration. [19] Daily routines were given

18. According to Mrs Schröder, Rietveld did not wish to have works by De Stijl artists in the Schröder house — although a work by Bart van der Leck appears in an early photograph. The walls, floors and ceilings were painted in different colours and greys, black and white, like the furniture, making works of art on the walls superfluous. The interior of the Schröder house became the total work of art that Mondrian dreamed of but was never able to achieve in his own work, apart perhaps from in the environment of his own studio. (See Nancy Troy, *The De Stijl Environment,* Cambridge, Massachusetts and London 1983, passim.) In 1919 Van Doesburg wrote of Rietveld's furniture: 'Through its new form, the furniture gives a new answer to the question of what place sculpture will have in the new interior. Our chairs, tables, cabinets and other objects of use are the (abstract-real) images of our future interior.' (*De Stijl,* Vol.2, No. 11, 1919, p.135.) This was the role that Rietveld's furniture was to assume in the interior of the Schröder house five years later. The chairs, tables and cabinets functioned as 'abstract-real' images, but at the same time remained objects for use. In this context — that of a very much lived-in space — they never quite became sculpture, operating in an area somewhere between use and symbolic function. (For further discussion of this see Paul Overy, 'Gerrit Rietveld: Furniture and Meaning', in *2D/3D: Art and Craft Made and Designed for the Twentieth Century,* exhibition catalogue, Laing Art Gallery, Newcastle; Northern Centre for the Arts, Sunderland 1987) In later years Mrs Schröder hung a few original paintings and reproductions in the house.

19. 'It was, as I now begin to see, the setting for a masque celebrating the arrival of a new style... a new wonder, played out there on the edge of a small town, facing the quiet fields.' Peter Smithson, 'For Truus Schröder-Schräder', in Alison and Peter Smithson, 1981, p.19, op.cit.

20. *De Stijl,* Vol.7, No.3-4, 1926, pp.29-30. (In English in the original.) See also a note from Van Doesburg's notebook dated 13th June 1928, published posthumously in the last issue of *De Stijl,* 1932, Vol.9, pp.21-22.

21. Colin St.John Wilson, *Architectural Review,* CXXXVI, Dec. 1964

significance by means of the specially designed equipment and built-in furniture; the interaction of space and matter was conceived as a process of revealing reality; and nature and culture were intimately related by breaking down the traditional divisions between outside and inside. But this was not to be a rarefied aesthetic life; instead the everyday and the ordinary were to be given a special meaning and significance which would raise them to the level of art. A year or two after the Schröder house was completed, Van Doesburg published a manifesto in De Stijl entitled 'The End of Art'. The Schröder house and the life that Mrs Schröder and Rietveld had envisaged being lived in it might be seen as the embodiment of this ideal although Van Doesburg's manifesto was written more from a Dadaist than a Constructivist or Neo-plasticist point of view whereas neither Rietveld nor Mrs Schröder would have positioned themselves in either theoretical camp despite their membership of De Stijl:

'One cannot renew Art. "Art" is an invention of the Renaissance which has today refined itself to the utmost degree possible. An enormous concentration was needed to make good works of Art. One could only develop this concentration by neglecting life (as in religion) or to lose life entirely. That is today impossible for we are only interested in life. (...) Let's refresh ourselves with things that are not Art: the bathroom, the W.C. the bathtub, the telescope, the bicycle, the auto, the subways, the flat-iron. There are many people who know how to make such good unartistic things. But they are hindered, and their movements are dictated, by the priests of Art. Art, whose function nobody knows, hinders the function of life. For the sake of progress we must destroy Art. Because the function of modern life is stronger than Art, every attempt to renew Art (Futurism, Cubism, Expressionism) failed. They are all bankrupt. Let us not waste our time with them. Let us rather create a new life-form which is adequate to the functioning of modern life.' [20]

Mrs Schröder insisted that every room or individual area which could be divided off by the sliding and folding partitions should be provided with a divan bed, separate washbasin and cooking facilities. This was not only for functional reasons; these were symbols of the daily rituals of living and imbued with an almost religious significance. The English architect Colin St. John Wilson has described the primal, 'mystic positivism' of the imagery of the Schröder house and its furniture and fittings:

'...the first chairs, the first light-fittings, table, cupboard, radio-set, desk, flexible walls — in short the first house and all the equipment in it to match the dream of a world in which only the New could be marvellous and desirable. (...) We are shamed today by an imagery so intense, so innocent and so defiant; and the further miracle is that two such small and unremarkable things as a chair and a house could condense such potential energy. (...) Its plastic rules were few and were formulated like a set of philosophical propositions about elements and their relations; their aim was to celebrate a way of life in which clarity and simplicity were articles of faith as much as they were constructive means; they were tools of a positivism claiming mystical insight.' [21]

Today this faith seems extraordinary. Yet it is moving to see its evidence restored in the reconstruction of the 1925 interior of the Schröder house.

Above: situation sketch. Drawing by Bertus Mulder, 1987
Left: view of southwest and southeast facade, c.1925
On the right is the former wooden shed

The site that Mrs Schröder and Rietveld found for the house was an awkward and difficult one, abutting a clumsy nondescript block of traditional Dutch brick-built apartment houses at the end of the Prins Hendriklaan, a suburban street which led from a pleasant park to the edge of the city. The advantage of the site was that immediately beyond was open countryside; it looked across polders with trees, meadows and canals. At the time these polders formed part of the old water defence system of Holland (they could be flooded in war-time) and building on them was prohibited. Thus it seemed to Mrs Schröder and Rietveld that the fine views the house enjoyed would be protected. Unfortunately, shortly after the house was built the law was changed, as the water defences were long outdated, and the land began to be developed in the late 1920s and 1930s.

The house had been orientated so that the main entrance and the facade with its wide, generous first floor windows faced not onto the Prins Hendriklaan but across the meadows. In 1939 a ring road was built passing close to this facade. In 1963 this was converted into a raised motorway. Today the windows that once looked across fields and trees face straight onto this motorway, which is approximately at the same level as the living area on the first floor. This happened shortly before Rietveld's death and his first instinct was to demolish the house. He said that he had never thought of his buildings being made to last for more than fifty years, and there is indeed a temporary and transient quality about much of his architectural work.[22] The perennial youthfulness of the Schröder house was often commented on by visitors. In 1964 Wilson wrote that 'after forty years it is still the youngest house in Europe'.[23] Even in Mrs Schröder's extreme old age the house still had a youthful quality. Its sense of newness never seemed to be diminished. Now, after its restoration, it is suspended in a state of eternal youth.

In the decades since it was built the apple trees in the small garden of the Schröder house have grown up and, in summer at least, provide some kind of visual screen against the motorway. (A glass sound barrier has recently been erected.) It is still possible with a little imagination to visualise how the building must have been when it faced across the countryside. Peter Smithson has described the sensations of a visitor to the house in Mrs Schröder's later years:
'Last year I went yet again to the last house on the left in Prins Hendriklaan in Utrecht.
The sun shone, the house sat there amongst its blossoming trees, enjoying its fifty-fifth year of life.
This house and I were born in the same year: as it matures, and in response to the small pleasures of its cottage garden, I begin to gather-up two small thoughts:
Firstly, how becoming to a house is the care an affection of its owner... especially so here, where the owner was patroness, inspirer, and joint-inventor.
Secondly, when it was new, how innocent this house. It is put together with

22. This was perhaps because his earliest commissions were for shop conversions which inevitably have only a short life. (None of these have survived.) Rietveld said that he prefered houses with scaffolding round them. (The Futurists had expressed similar sentiments in their manifestos.) One of Rietveld's chairs of the late 1920s was constructed from scaffolding poles clamped together.

23. Dec. 1964, op.cit.

nailed 2 x 1 battens and paint, as if for some celebration; as if it need not last as the houses beside it were intended to last.
It was, as I now begin to see, the setting for a masque celebrating the arrival of a new style...a new wonder, played out there on the edge of a small town, facing the quiet fields.' [24]

Utrecht is no longer a quiet town but a substantial city with a great deal of ugly post-war architecture, most of it far from the ideal of Rietveld's early work. Nonetheless the compactness of the Schröder house, its sense of quiet enjoyment, and the intimate light spaces of the first floor interior, can invoke in the visitor something of the qualities the house had when first built and continued to have during Mrs Schröder's lifetime, despite the growth of the city beyond and the gross intrusion of the motorway.

By banishing conventional decorative features and ornament from the exterior and interior, early modernist architecture aimed to establish a symbiosis with nature in its place. Instead of ornament which imitated nature, real nature was incorporated into the building or its immediate ambiance. Hence the roof gardens of Le Corbusier and the cantilevered projecting balconies of almost all modern movement domestic architecture of the 1920s and 1930s. More than any other early 20th century domestic building the Schröder house achieves this symbiosis. The large windows on the first floor, which once looked across the countryside and now look onto the trees in the small garden, are designed to open outwards and visually extend the living space into the space outside, at the same time channelling the air and (almost it seems) the branches and leaves of the trees into the space of the interior, creating a strange but exhilarating sensation of being suspended between nature and human habitation.
Inside the house Mrs Schröder liked to place a few carefully chosen flowers. (These can even be seen in the early black and white photographs of 1925.) The organic forms of nature seen through  the windows, or discreetly arranged in vases inside the house, contrast with and provide a foil for the plain, smooth geometric surfaces of the interior walls, painted in primary colours or neutral greys.

The trees in the garden work in a similar way with the planes of the exterior walls which appear to be separate from each other, as moveable as the sliding partitions inside. (Mrs Schröder recalled that when the house was first built people came to stare at it waiting for the walls to collapse like a house of cards.) As the garden has matured over the years these trees have come to substitute for the vista of meadows and canals which originally extended to the east of the house. One tree in particular has a very strong relationship to the exterior. In the early black and white photographs this can be seen as a young sapling outlined against the white plane of the wall which faces onto Prins Hendriklaan. Today this tree has grown into a gnarled and dense organic structure which — particularly in winter — resembles the tree which Mondrian painted again and again in his early years and on which some of his early abstractions were based. The whole of this Prins Hendriklaan facade has often been compared to Mondrian's abstract

First floor, c.1925; view of the boy's room showing the grand piano that stood in the original interior. In the photograph left, the film projector standing on the Stacking cabinet, 1925

24. Peter Smithson, 'For Truus Schröder-Schräder', in Alison and Peter Smithson, 1981, p.19, op.cit.

paintings of the early 1920s although Rietveld almost certainly arrived at his architectural composition of lines, colour and planes independently.[25]

Inside the house colour was used, particularly in the upper living area, as a way of articulating the space, of controlling the play of light, and of creating a sense of brightness and enjoyment. Rietveld seems to have first used colour in the furniture and toys he made for children.[26] He himself had six children, born between 1916 and 1924, the key years of his own development from furniture-maker to architect. The Schröder house was designed not only for Mrs Schröder but also for her children: colour was used most freely in the upper parts of the house where they had their own rooms in the early years of the house's life.

When the house was first occupied, the sliding and folding partitions were often closed to create separate rooms for the children. The two girls, Marjan and Han, shared one room with a window overlooking Prins Hendriklaan.The son, Binnert, the eldest, had a room to himself with windows looking out across the country. The three divan beds could be converted into couches scattered with red, yellow and blue cushions, and the partitions folded back when the whole of the upper floor space needed to be used for family gatherings or to entertain visitors.[27] Mrs Schröder had a bedroom scarcely larger than the small double bed itself, next to the bathroom. This room was turned into a kitchenette when the house was altered in 1936, and Mrs Schröder slept on a divan in the first floor living area after the children had left home.

The dining area was the main focus of the first floor, situated at the angle of the wide-opening windows which originally looked across the countryside. With its 'disappearing corner', this remains the most spectacular and dramatic part of the house.[28] It was also the centre of family life when the Schröder children were teenagers. There was a sloping shelf beside the table, facing across the fields, designed for them to do their homework. (This was removed after the children grew up, but has now been restored.) Here Mrs Schröder used to receive her visitors in later years and make coffee or tea. People who came to the house would naturally gravitate to this spot; for it is here that the inside-outside character of the upper floor of the house is most lyrically manifest. In winter, spring, autumn or summer, this is always the most magical area of the house. It manages to triumph over the motorway outside which even in summer is never completely masked by the trees.

The only fixed areas of the upper floor are the staircase itself, the wc and bathroom and the stove and chimney column, which is close to the staircase, free-standing in the centre of the upper floor. This creates a central area of stability, a 'core' around which the transformable spaces are grouped.[29] The sliding partitions which enable the space of the upper floor to be divided off into four separate rooms were made of bitumenized cork sandwiched between beaver board. They run in recessed grooves at floor level and 'T' sections of steel guide them at the ceiling.[30] These partitions can be closed

25. Brown, 1958, pp.61-64, op.cit.

26. In children's furniture of c.1918 and a cradle painted red and yellow and lined with blue fabric for his son Jan in 1919. He made a Child's wheelbarrow and a Baby buggy around 1923 which were painted in the De Stijl primary colours as was the End Table of the same year. It was probably then that the Red Blue chair was first painted. (See Marijke Küper, in Blotkamp (et. al.), 1982, p.272 ff, op.cit.)

27. '... the intention (...) is that the interior can be altered daily according to the changing needs of the different times of the day and night. I doubt that this extreme flexibility and changeability will seem convenient in the long run. That does not alter the fact, however, that a certain amount of changeability of arrangement, especialy for the small house, can be very desirable ...' (J.G.Wattjes, 'Moderne bouwkunst in Utrecht', *Het Bouwbedrijf*, Sept.1925; quoted in Brown, 1958, p.57, original Dutch, pp. 155-56, note 43, op.cit.)

28. At the point where the windows meet at the east corner of the house, Rietveld displaced the steel I-beam supporting the roof about a foot, so that when the windows are flung wide open the glazed corner 'disappears' and the transparent planes of the windows seem to catch the fresh air and the foliage of the trees outside and channel them into the interior of the house.

Interior and exterior of the 'Row-houses', number 5-11, Erasmuslaan, designed by Rietveld and Mrs Schröder in 1930-31

29. The original fireplace was brought, like the bath, from the house in the Biltstraat. Later this was replaced by a plainer, freestanding stove. This remains in the house after the restoration as the original fireplace has been destroyed. In the period 1929-58 Rietveld made several designs for 'core' housing, where the essential services would be centrally grouped, to which prefabricated rooms could be attached according to requirements. These were never built.

30. Brown, 1958 p.55, op.cit.

31. The Stacking cabinet had long been dismantled, but Bertus Mulder found parts of it in the cellar and had it reconstructed. The built-in furniture and equipment was executed by Rietveld's assistant, Van de Groenekan, who lived in the house while working on the interior. Van de Groenekan had been apprenticed to Rietveld as a furniture-maker, and took over Rietveld's furniture business from 1924 until he went to South Africa in 1937. On his return after the war he continued to make furniture for Rietveld, and to order after Rietveld's death until 1971 when the rights were sold to the Italian firm Cassina. Van de Groenekan still restores Rietveld furniture and makes pieces on commission for museums.

32. This has been preserved after the restoration of the house and installed in the study centre next door.

or half closed, making different combinations of open, closed or half-open spaces. When Mrs Schröder's children lived in the house, the partitions tended to be closed to give them privacy. After they left home the partitions were usually kept open. In later years Mrs Schröder left them open during the day and closed them at night.

Most of the built-in furniture in the house was designed for this transformable first floor space: wardrobes and cupboards for the children's toys and clothes, and a washbasin unit in a cupboard in Mrs Schröder's bedroom. But the most original and spectacular piece was a storage unit consisting of a number of different sized stacking boxes arranged like a constructivist sculpture, each unit visually discrete, as are the elements of Rietveld's early furniture like the Red Blue chair and the Buffet, but composed in an asymmetric structure closer to the Berlin chair and End table that he had designed in 1923. The boxes slid apart and opened in an ingenious way like a Rubik cube. One contained a gramophone and in early photographs of the house a film projector can be seen standing on one of these boxes. [31]

In 1936 Mrs Schröder moved for a year into one of the apartments designed by Rietveld and herself opposite the Schröder house on the corner of the Erasmuslaan and the continuation of Prins Hendriklaan. While she was living there a number of alterations were made to the Schröder house. A small kitchenette was installed in what had originally been Mrs Schröder's bedroom. [32] A new built-in 'granito' hip-bath and washbasin was fitted into the bathroom in place of the old-fashioned bath which had been brought from the house in the Biltstraat. A small attic room was built for Mrs Schröder's use on the top of the house reached by an elegant metal staircase from the first floor. (This room was removed in the 1950s, but the staircase remained until the early 1970s.) With the staircase in place it was no longer possible to completely fold away the glass and wood partitions designed so that they could either close the stairwell off or be opened out to leave the space above it free.

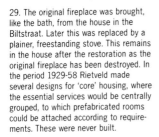

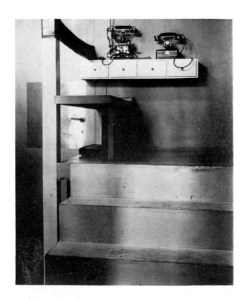

The ground floor of the Schröder house is quite different in character from the first floor, divided into four or five quite small rooms. The room facing onto Prins Hendriklaan was at first intended to be a garage, but in the final design became a studio used by Mrs Schröder and Rietveld, with a small workroom behind. [33] There is a separate exterior door to the studio from Prins Hendriklaan. The room at the south corner of the house is very small and was designed as a study or reading room, with built-in shelves and desk, and furnished with the red Armchair of 1925. Although many alterations were made to other parts of the house, this room was never changed, and has required little restoration. Its window looks onto the garden and originally would have had a view to the meadows and canals beyond; it also has its own door leading out into the garden. Outside, beside the door is a blue bench for sitting and enjoying the garden in summer.

The main front door is on this side of the house because Rietveld and Mrs Schröder thought that the Laan van Minsweerd, which approached Prins Hendriklaan from the southwest, would later be extended past the garden of the house. In fact this did not happen and eventually the motorway was built a few metres further on. The front door is divided in two horizontally, like a barn or stable door — a feature of traditional Dutch houses in the countryside. Beside this is a cupboard glazed with opaque glass combining a letter box and shelves for the children to store toys used outdoors. The front door opens into the hall, which was not changed over the years. To the left is an open fitted cupboard and shelves for outdoor coats, hats, shoes etc. with a small radiator underneath to dry them off. This cupboard has no door. Four steps lead onto the half-landing where there is a telephone shelf with drawers beneath and a bench seat with a simple leather strap back-rest. From the half-landing a tightly angled staircase leads up to the first floor.

To the right of the hall is the original kitchen of the house. This was big

33. Mrs Schröder never owned a car.
Rietveld owned one after the war.

Ground floor, c.1925
Left: main entrance with top door open. Beside it, the glass protruding cupboard with a small letter box and shelves for toys used outdoors
Above: kitchen, with the shelf for deliveries and shopping near the window

enough for four people to eat in; a service lift was provided to take food prepared downstairs up to the first floor dining area for more formal eating and entertaining. Behind the kitchen was a small maid's room. This was designed to take a bed; but in practice Mrs Schröder never had a living-in maid, only a woman who came in by the day.[34] To the left of the long kitchen window is a small shelf for the tradesmen to leave deliveries.

Emerging from the relative darkness of the hall and ground floor rooms into the brilliance and light of the first floor is like going up onto the upper deck of a ship. The contrast between the light, open upper floor and the closed, separate, darker private rooms of the ground floor allowed the inhabitants of the house to choose between enclosed privacy or a more communal openness. However, although the rooms on the ground floor are small and enclosed, there are window strips at the top of the communicating walls between the study, the wc (to the right of the hall) and the original kitchen, which provide extra light in the hall and create a visual link between the private spaces of these enclosed rooms and the more public space of hall and stairs. Inside the rooms one is aware of the ceiling extending beyond their walls.

Holland is one of the most crowded countries in the world. Hence privacy is much valued. But it is a 'social privacy'. Long ago the Dutch arrived at a concept of privacy that is not isolating to the point of loneliness. If one walks down a Dutch street at night one notices that the front rooms are impeccable, the lights are on and the curtains remain undrawn. These rooms are both 'private' and 'public'. The balance between openness and privacy

34. Binnert and Marjan Schröder, in conversation with the author, 13 Feb. 1987

35. After leaving elementary school in 1900, Rietveld worked — although not in one continious stretch — until 1917 in his father's furniture-making business. This firm was well-known in Utrecht for its faithful copies of traditional styles of furniture. One of Rietveld's other employers during this period was the jeweler Begeer. Between 1904-08 Rietveld attended evening school at the local college for applied arts, where he had the reputation of being a very good student. From about 1906, for several years he attended evening classes given by the architect P.J.C. Klaarhamer, whose work was similar to Berlage's. Qualifying as an architect by part-time study of this kind was much more common everywhere in Europe in the early 20th century than it is now. (N.B. Accounts of Rietveld's early training and activities vary, see Brown, 1958, op.cit.; Marijke Küper, in Blotkamp (et.al.), 1982, op.cit; Frits Bless, Rietveld 1888-1964. Een biografie, Amsterdam/Baarn 1982)

36. El Lissitzky, 'Architecture, Housing Culture', Stroitel' naia Promyshlennost, No.12, Dec.1926; quoted in Brown, 1958, p.58, op.cit.; quoted in Mildred Friedman (ed.), De Stijl 1917-1931, Visions of Utopia, Minneapolis / New York 1982, p.139

37. Brian Housden, 'Jolly Nice Furniture: A note on the work of Gerrit Thomas Rietveld' in 2D/3D: Art and Craft Made and Designed for the Twentieth Century, exhibition catalogue, 1987, p.54, op.cit. The Stedelijk Museum, Amsterdam has an extensive collection of Rietveld's models.

which is one of the most important features of the Schröder house is an adaptation of this traditional feature to new modes of living. Light is perceived as a molding and shaping force in the interior spaces of the house and there is an extraordinary sense of calm and peace, a sense of being both enclosed and free. One is inside, yet at all times aware of the outside beyond the walls and windows. And, from inside, the large windows which let in the outside world are like pictures which open onto the world. (Such windows are now popularly called 'picture windows' in English.)

---

Rietveld was a furniture-maker by trade, and although he had studied architecture and design at evening classes, he had only worked on shop and interior conversions before 1924.[35] Because of his early practice as a *maker* rather than as a designer Rietveld usually worked with cardboard or paper models in designing furniture and in the first stages of architectural commissions. After visiting the Schröder house in 1926, the Russian artist and designer El Lissitzky wrote of Rietveld: 'He does all with models, feeling things with his hands; and therefore his product is not abstract'. As a result, Lissitzky pointed out: 'one cannot judge such works by photographs, since by photographs we see only a view and not the life of the form'.[36] Rietveld continued to work in this way until the end of his life, even on large scale commissions. The English architect Brian Housden recalled visiting Rietveld in the Schröder house in his later years:
'On a table at the side of Rietveld's bed and on other tables at the side of the chair he occupied and near to the place where he ate, were neatly grouped a pile of small pieces of paper and card, a pot of glue, a pair of scissors and a small box of crayons. Wherever Rietveld was and under every possible circumstance, except when he was having a bath, he had only to stretch out his hand to find a piece of card which he could shape into the miniature form of a piece of furniture or part of a building or even an entire

Rietveld in the 1950s

building. Whereas most architects keep a sketchbook in which they note down buildings or parts of buildings that interest them and subsequently incorporate the information into their own "new" designs. Rietveld was unique in his generation of European architects for designing straight from his own imagination in three dimensions to scale instantaneously. His tiny models, once made, in the case of a piece of furniture, would then be translated into a cutting schedule, that would then be handed to a wood machine shop. The parts required then machined and cut to length and returned to Rietveld for assembly. The process from conception of the design to finished product taking no more than 8 hours.' [37]

It is important, however, not to perpetuate a myth of Rietveld as a simple untutored craftsman turned architect and designer. [38] This tendency to characterise Rietveld as 'a simple carpenter' began at least as early as Lissitzky's description of the Schröder house, where he wrote that: 'He is not an architectural student, he is a carpenter, and he was not able routinely to draw out a plan'. [39] Although Rietveld continued to work with models throughout his life he was perfectly capable of drawing out a plan. And while it is true that he was, in Peter Smithson's words, 'an architect of the rarest sort — an architect of manual intuition', [40] he was not just a simple and naive carpenter. It is understandable that in a Soviet publication of the mid-1920s Lissitzky should want to suggest that 'the house was the product of a proletarian imagination'. More recent attempts to mythologize Rietveld as a simple and unlettered craftsman are less excusable. However there were important ways in which his practice as a furniture designer and architect differed markedly from other furniture designers and architects of the modern movement as Brian Housden described above. [41]

The 'manual intuition' Rietveld had gained as a furniture-*maker* meant that he tended to visualise his designs in terms of three dimensional models rather than conceptually in terms of two dimensional drawings. [42] Unlike most architects his training in architectural drawing came *after* he had already established a strong working practice of 'thinking manually'. Because the Schröder house was the first complete building Rietveld designed, it was planned and put together like a piece of furniture. And just as furniture, and in particular a chair, is scaled to the human form, so the house is scaled to human dimensions. The early furniture by Rietveld with which the Schröder house was furnished served as a kind of measure of the human scale within the house.

As a furniture-maker Rietveld had been used to making objects which inhabit the interior of architecture. Between 1918, when he made the first version of the Red Blue chair, and 1923, when he made the asymmetrical Berlin chair (constructed almost entirely from flat planes), he developed the symbolic function of the chair from that of a sculptural metaphor — an anthropomorphic image, a symbol of the seated human figure, containing space like the human body itself — to that of architectural metaphor. Many 20th century architects have designed furniture, but very few furniture-makers have become architects. (Marcel Breuer is another, but none of his

38. Daniele Baroni, *The Furniture of Gerrit Thomas Rietveld*, London 1979, p.29; Martin Filler, 'The Furniture of Gerrit Rietveld: Manifestos for a New Revolution' in Mildred Friedman (ed.), 1982, p.126, op.cit.

39. Quoted in Brown, 1958, p.57, op.cit.

40. Peter Smithson, 'Rietveld', *Architectural Design*, Sept.1964, reprinted in Alison and Peter Smithson, 1981, p.18, op.cit.

41. His ideas developed from practice rather than theory, just as in designing buildings or furniture he often worked from models rather than the more conceptual method of drawing. Much of Rietveld's work of the period immediately after the completion of the Schröder house was done in collaboration with Mrs Schröder, who also helped to finance this. Rietveld published a number of articles and statements about his work and his approach to design; the majority of these were written after he had designed the Schröder house. Rietveld was undoubtedly influenced by Mrs Schröder's ideas and encouragement; it was probably through her influence that he began to read more widely and write extensively himself. There are over seventy published pieces by Rietveld and 'countless unpublished fragments'. (Theodore M.Brown, 'Rietveld's Egocentric Vision', *Journal of the Society of Architectural Historians*, Dec. 1965, Vol. XXIV, No.4, p.292) Brown's article includes quotations from some of Rietveld's writings translated into English, and a selected bibliography. Brown's monograph on Rietveld (1958, op.cit.) contains the Dutch text and translations of an article of 1928 and a recorded statement of 1957. Four texts dating from 1939 to 1963 are published (in Dutch only) in Helma van Rens (ed.), *Gerrit Rietveld Teksten*, Utrecht 1979. The Dutch texts of one article (1939) and three lectures or speeches made by Rietveld towards the end of his life are reprinted in Frits Bless, 1982, pp.220-48, op.cit.

42. Two models were used in the design of the Schröder house: a solid wood model in which the design of the house appears very cubic, lacking the apparently independent planes of the final design, and a later model put together from cardboard, glass and matchsticks, (destroyed) where the elements of the final design were tried out. However some of these elements are apparent in a drawing by Rietveld which may precede this later model. Rietveld seems in practice to have designed by means of a combination of models and sketches.

Hanging lamp, c.1922, photographed in the Rietveld Schröder House, c.1925. The way in which it was attached to the ceiling was later changed, and this change was retained in the 1986-87 restoration (see ill. pp.82-83, 98-99, 102)

chairs — not even the brilliant Wassily tubular chair of 1925 — has become such a seminal artifact as Rietveld's Red Blue chair. Nor do any of Breuer's buildings have the intensity of the Schröder house.) Rietveld designed the house in the same way as the Red Blue chair, stripping it down to the elements from which it is made (legs, seat, back / walls, floors, ceilings) and putting these together in a new, dramatic, and surprising way.

The chair was designed to be mass produced, although it never has been. [43] It is, however, quite easy to make and many architects, designers, students and amateur carpenters have knocked together their own versions of the Red Blue chair. Not only is Rietveld furniture relatively easy to 'do it yourself' — it also *looks* easy to make. This quality is carried over into the design of the Schröder house, which looks as though one could build it oneself, as if 'put together with nailed 2 x 1 battens and paint'. [44]

Rietveld is often misleadingly described as a cabinet-maker by trade. Although as a young man he had done cabinet-making for his father — high quality, highly-skilled work using veneers and expensive woods — his practice was mainly carpentry and furniture-making (where the wood was cut by machine) or shop- and interior-fitting. [45] Rietveld undoubtedly had much of the craftsman's approach and attitudes (in his 'manual' approach to design, for example) but he did not exalt craftsmanship for its own sake. With his particular background and training, where skilled craftsmanship was combined with the more straightforward and easily learned accomplishments of carpentry and wood-machining, Rietveld was able to perceive the falsity of the aura which had come to surround craftsmanship as the result of the influence of William Morris and the Arts and Crafts movement. (In Holland craft and machine practice were much less separated in the early decades of the century than in England.)

In his statements about the design and construction of pieces like the Red Blue chair it is clear that Rietveld conceived these as a deliberate assault on the mystique of craftsmanship. [46] However, unlike many of the designers of the 1920s and 1930s, Rietveld's designs do not fetishize machine production. They retain a clumsy and awkward quality which give them their peculiar charm, as if avoiding the perfect smoothness of machine products — which is itself a mystification, for machine production leaves a product with rough edges which have to be milled and polished, in the case of metal, or sanded and sealed or painted, in the case of wood. [47] Rietveld began to make his early furniture at just that point when machine methods of wood cutting were being introduced into furniture-making and the methods and traditions of the craftsman were being challenged. Hence the ambiguity of his early pieces, which are designed to be machine-cut and assembled in quantity, but yet to retain a look of the hand-made about them. Because of their often deliberate oddity of construction they never become anonymous machine products.

Before setting up on his own as a furniture-maker Rietveld was for some years a draughtsman with Cornelis Begeer, one of the leading jewelers in

43. The first version of the Red Blue chair, as yet unpainted, was first published in the magazine *De Stijl,* Vol.2, No.11, 1919, pp. 438-39, entitled: 'Armchair by Rietveld' (see ill. p.48). It was not painted in the familiar De Stijl colours of red, yellow, blue and black until about 1923. (See Marijke Küper, in Blotkamp (et.al.), 1982, pp. 259-77, op.cit.)

44. Peter Smithson, in Alison and Peter Smithson, 1981, p.19, op.cit. A book on how to make Rietveld furniture has been published: *Rietveld Meubels Om Zelf Te Maken: Werkboek / How To Construct Rietveld Furniture: Workbook,* (text in Dutch and English), Delft 1986. Model kits for various pieces of Rietveld furniture and for the Schröder house are also on sale with instructions in Dutch and English and several other languages. Rietveld, however, always refused to have the Schröder house exhibited as a model at Madurodam — where famous Dutch buildings are re-created in miniature — because he said it had to be experienced as reality, at its proper scale, and not in miniature. (Marjan Schröder, in conversation with the author, 13 Feb. 1987)

45. I am indebted to Brian Housden, who owns an exemplary collection of Rietveld furniture, for making clear these distinctions.

46. See interview, note 18

47. This was certainly true in the 1920s and is still largely true today although it is now possible to obtain better quality finishes by machine. The chromed tubular chairs of the 1920s required a great deal of hand finishing and were hence always expensive and never really 'mass produced'.

Holland.[48] Some of his first commissions (and one of his last in 1963) were remodelling jewelers' shops. Rietveld's experience as a jewelery designer is often ignored. Yet his best work has a jewel-like quality as well as the plainness of artisanal furniture-making. For the remodelling of the G. & Z.C. jewelry shop in Amsterdam — one of his most remarkable early commissions — Rietveld designed the shop front as a series of independent, asymmetrically stacked glass display cases. On top of these he placed a twenty-sided 'diamond' made of mirror glass with an electric light inside which would gleam at night and draw the attention of the passer-by to the window display.[49] Inside the shop he designed light fittings where bare electric light bulbs were clustered together like pearls. The lamp constructed of three small Philips strip lights which hangs in the Schröder house[50] is like a jewel embedded in the plain setting of the carpentered interior of the first floor living space, which is often quite roughly finished.[51]

It was these particular qualities of Rietveld's work — avoiding the self-conscious craftsmanship or the luxury of hand-production while at the same time retaining his 'manual intuition' and jeweler's insight — that must have appealed to Mrs Schröder. This accorded with her own ideas about creating a distinctive environment in which to live and bring up her family. It must not be impersonal — in fact it was to be highly personalised. But unlike most custom-made interiors of the 19th century and of the first decades of the 20th century, it was not intended to signify class, luxury, and inherited or acquired wealth. Rather it was to proclaim new ways of living well, in which an appearance of purity, healthiness, fresh air and light was of prime importance. This is a quality the Schröder house shares with many of the buildings of the early modernist period. Like the lighter, more comfortable, less voluminous and less luxurious looking clothes adopted by middle class women in Western Europe after the First World War, modern architecture inscribed an optimistic belief in the mental and physical health-giving properties of design.

As well as its own specially made equipment and fittings, the Schröder house was furnished with some of Rietveld's early furniture. These pieces occupied a privileged position in the interior because of their direct relationship to it. Later Mrs Schröder also had furniture that Rietveld designed after the house was built, such as the Zig-Zag (or Z) chair of 1934 and the Steltman chair of 1963, one of Rietveld's last works. The open design of the Schröder house could incorporate such changes, modifications and refurbishings. In Mrs Schröder's lifetime the house was a record of these changes and of the life that had been lived in it. No restoration could possibly preserve this, although photographs record something of the house as it was in Mrs Schröder's last years.

---

Both the Red Blue chair and the Schröder house are designed to show that they are clearly constructed from separate elements: pieces of machined wood in the case of the chair, the planes of walls, roof, floors in the house.

48. Rietveld designed a ring for Mrs Schröder's eldest daughter, Marjan Schröder, in the 1950s.

49. Brown, 1958, p.26, ill. p.25, op.cit.

50. This was first designed for Dr A.M. Hartog's surgery in Maarssen in 1922.

51. In restoring and reconstructing the built-in furniture Bertus Mulder deliberately used carpenters rather than cabinet-makers, and had to restrain them from finishing it to too high a standard. As Peter Smithson has written, the house was 'put together with nailed 2x1 battens and paint, as if for some celebration; as if it need not last as the houses beside it were intended to last.' (Peter Smithson, in Alison and Peter Smithson, 1981, p.19, op.cit.)

Rietveld had already arrived at a way of designing using simplified elements when he made the Red Blue chair, the Buffet and the Child's High chair around 1918 (all of which were illustrated in *De Stijl* in 1919).[52] In these early pieces Rietveld reduced the design to a construction of machine cut wooden elements which could be put together like children's building blocks. In the Buffet he explored the idea of using cantilevered planes, which have a certain resemblance to early Frank Lloyd Wright houses like the Robie House in Chicago, which Rietveld knew from photographs.[53]

In the Berlin chair and End table, which Rietveld designed in 1923 just before the Schröder house, he explored the use of planes in an almost constructivist manner. The main difference between these two pieces of funiture and the Red Blue chair and Buffet is that, as well as being planar rather than elemental, they are completely asymmetric. Asymmetry is one of the most paradigmatic characteristics of the Schröder house, as of almost all modernist domestic architecture of the 1920s, inscribing an ideology of the informal.

By the time Rietveld came to design and build the Schröder house he was familiar with the ideas about space and architecture of Van Doesburg who regarded the house as the embodiment of these ideas in built form. It is often considered to be the only extant building which incorporates the ideals and formal innovations of De Stijl. However its design was not program-matic, but pragmatic. More than the manifesto it is often claimed to be, it represented a way of life. As such it was not static but continually changed. 'I did not think that function as a point of departure was a sound approach', Rietveld said later. 'Function was an accidental, casual need that would change with the time and indeed always changes in the course of time.'[54] The house was designed so that it could be adapted to accommodate Mrs Schröder's changing needs as her young family grew up and eventually left home. It became the living record of the life of a family and of the remarkable collaboration between patron and designer.
Rietveld's early furniture is clearly not functional in the way in which the metal furniture of the late 1920s appears to be functional (although no object, not even an 'object of use', can be *purely* functional). He clearly saw the limitations of functionalism and realised that the designer creates symbolic forms as much as usable objects.

In the design of the exterior of the Schröder house Rietveld was influenced not only by his own earlier furniture such as the Red Blue chair and the Buffet, and by more recent pieces like the Berlin chair and the End Table of 1923, but also by the architectural projects which Van Doesburg and the young architect Cornelis van Eesteren prepared for the De Stijl exhibition at Leonce Rosenberg's Galerie L'Effort Moderne in Paris in 1923. These projects — themselves incorporating many of the ideas already apparent in Rietveld's earlier furniture — were 'ideal' architecture, planar and construc-tivist, and as such never could have been and were never intended to be realised.[55]

52. Van Doesburg's theory of Elementarism, formulated when he began to use diagonal elements extens-ively in his work c. 1924-25 was a much more conceptual approach than that of Rietveld who remained always guided by his 'manual intuition'. For a discussion of elementarism seen in a wider context as one of the key issues in architecture, painting and design in the 1910s and 1920s, see Reyner Banham, *Theory and Design in the First Machine Age,* London 1960, p.187 ff. For Van Doesburg's ideas on Elementarism, see, 'Painting and plastic art : Elementarism' *De Stijl,* Vol.7, No. 78, 1927, and 'Elementarism and its origins', *De Stijl* Vol.8, No. 87/89, 1928, translated in Joost Baljeu, *Theo Van Doesburg,* London 1974, pp.163-75

53. In 1918 Rietveld had been asked to design furniture in the style of Wright for a villa at Huis ter Heide near Utrecht designed by Robert van 't Hoff, an early member of De Stijl who had met Wright in the USA.

54. Quoted in *G. Rietveld Architect,* exhibition catalogue, 1971/1972, np., op.cit.

55. Rietveld made the model for one of these, the Hotel Particulier. This was painted white rather than in the De Stijl primary colours and arrived late. The Hotel Particulier was the first of Van Doesburg and Van Eesteren's designs; the later Maison Particulière and Maison d'Artiste were more abstract and 'ideal'.

56. El Lissitzky, 1926, op.cit.; quoted in Brown, 1958, p.58, op.cit.; quoted in Mildred Friedman (ed.), 1982, p.139, op.cit.

57. De Stijl, Vol.5, No.10-11 (special double number devoted to El Lissitzky)

58. Reproductions and photographs of avant-garde work from Soviet Russia were circulating freely in the West by 1922. Malevich claimed a suprematist influence on Rietveld's design for Dr Hartog's surgery in Maarsen of 1922. (Kasimir Malevich, Essays on Art 1915-1933, Troels Andersen (ed.), 1969, Vol.II, p.83; ill.69,70.) In 1919 Rietveld had signed a petition to the Dutch parliament protesting at the goverment's refusal to transmit mail to and from Soviet Russia. (Ger Harmsen, 'De Stijl and the Russian Revolution', in Mildred Friedman (ed.), 1982, pp.46-47, op.cit. Rietveld designed the cover for the bulletin of the Nederland-Nieuw Rusland Genootschap (Netherlands-New Russia Society), Sept.-Oct. 1928, of which he was a member. It is likely that the film projector, clearly visible in early photo-graphs of the interior of the Schröder house standing on the Stacking cabinet Rietveld designed for the first floor living space, was used to show the early Soviet films of Eisenstein, Pudovkin and Vertov to Mrs Schröder's friends. (See Frits Bless, 1982, p.82, op.cit.)

59. Congrès Internationaux d'Archi-tecture Moderne. One of the main mediums of propaganda for International Style architecture. (See CIAM, Interna-tional, Housing Town Planning, exhibition catalogue Rijksmuseum Kröller Müller Otterlo, Delft/Otterlo 1983 (text in Dutch and English)

60. Reyner Banham's view that Rietveld's only significant works were the Red Blue chair and the Schröder house seems untenable: 'No one, not even his official biographer, Theodore M.Brown, has yet been able to suggest why this very competent, but otherwise unremarkable provincial figure should twice have contributed such sympto-matic objects to the rise of the Modern Movement.' (Guide to Modern Archi-tecture, London 1962, p.56) As a corrective see Peter Smithson: 'From his first great work — the Red Blue chair in 1917, Rietveld made strike after strike of the purest genius. Without him the spirit of De Stijl would have been still-born as far as actual construction is concerned. Everyone can make his own list of Rietveld master-works from the Heroic Period: The Red Blue chair, 1917. The "incomparable house at Utrecht — the only truly canonical building in Northern Europe" (Rietveld/Schröder house) 1923-24. The glass radio cabinet that broke, 1925. The chauffeur's house at Utrecht, the best panel-construction house yet, 1927-28. The "G" shop in

Mrs Schröder and Rietveld managed to resolve the contradiction between ideal architecture and a more flexible functionalism by inscribing into the fabric of the Schröder house the intended — and later the actual — life style of its inhabitants. Rietveld said that only Mrs Schröder could have lived in the Schröder house. For although it was the first truly flexible dwelling which took into account the increased informality and freedom of social and living arrangements in the 20th century, yet at the same time, as a prototype for a new way of living, it clearly placed enormous demands on its occupants.

The Schröder house embodies a powerful symbolism inherent in its capacity — like the Red Blue chair — to be perceived both as a whole and as the sum of its individual parts. The Schröder house is put together like a piece of furniture, but at the same time it is planned like a town or a city, as Lissitzky perceived when he visited it in 1926: 'The entire upper floor presents itself as one huge room in which the furniture, with the exception of the chairs, is closely arranged: cupboards, beds, sofa-beds and tables are arranged like houses in a town in such a way that there are areas for movement and use as if they were streets and squares'.[56] Thus the Schröder house fulfills Alberti's ideal that the house was a small city and the city a large house. The house, like the chair, can therefore act as a potent symbol of human society: formally, in its 'unity in plurality', and functionally, as an interior which can be either opened or closed, preserving individual privacy or encouraging a more social interaction.

Such ideals and principles were shared by architects, artists and designers in the early years of the Soviet Union in Russia and it is not surprising that Lissitzky should have written about the house enthusiastically. Rietveld undoubtedly knew the work of the suprematists and constructivists from photographic reproductions and prints which circulated in the West in the early 1920s. Van Doesburg printed a Dutch version of Lissitzky's A Story of Two Squares in the De Stijl magazine in 1922.[57] And in one early photo-graph of the house a Lissitzky print or reproduction can be seen pinned to the bathroom door. Although Rietveld's early furniture designs like the Red Blue chair and the Buffet of c. 1918 undoubtedly resemble suprematist and constructivist paintings and constructions, they were certainly made before he could have seen photographs or reproductions of any such Russian work. But some of the built-in furniture and equipment made for the Schröder house may well have been partly inspired by Russian examples which both Rietveld and Mrs Schröder would have seen in magazines or photographs.[58]

In the late 1920s and early 1930s Rietveld began to work in the Neue Sachlichkeit or International Style. (He was an early member of CIAM.)[59] Although his work always remained sensitively and humanly scaled, manual intuition is less marked in his buildings of this period, which are more strictly functional and less individual. In the late 1920s Rietveld also designed furniture which made some attempts to conform to contemporary ideas about functionalism, although even these pieces remain oddly stylised compared with the more anonymous work of other designers of the period.

Germany, 1929. The row-houses opposite the Rietveld/Schröder house — the purest emanation of the Sachlichkeit spirit, 1930-31. Zig-Zag chair, 1934. All these works had a profound influence on *all* other architects. He influenced their form direct without rationalisation, even without their knowing it.' (*Architectural Design,* Sept. 1964, reprinted in Alison and Peter Smithson, 1981, p.17, op.cit. The dates given for Rietveld's works here are not always quite accurate)

61. Dec. 1964, op.cit.

62. However Van Doesburg too, despite his enormous faith in technology (which he saw as spiritually redemptive), realised that the designer creates symbolic forms as much as usable objects, opposing the hard-line German constructivists associated with the Berlin magazine *G* and Dutch architect-designers like Mart Stam, whose position was close to that of the Russian 'productivists'.

63. The De Stijl group was held together largely through the magazine *De Stijl* and the personality of Van Doesburg; the members did not meet as a group and most of their contact was through correspondence.

64. Peter Smithson, in Alison and Peter Smithson, 1981, p.19, op.cit.

Manual intuition is, however, clearly apparent in many of the country villas that constituted Rietveld's main architectural practice from the mid-1930s to the early 1940s, and in particular those designed as summer houses in rural parts of Holland. And it is an essential element in the conception and design of much of his furniture of the mid-1930s such as the Zig-Zag (or Z) chair and the Crate furniture which was originally designed for summer or weekend houses and sold flat to be assembled by the purchaser. Works like these were the direct descendants of the Red Blue chair and the Schröder house although they were less individualistic and idiosyncratic. [60]

Colin St. John Wilson described the Schröder house and its equipment as the first 'to match the dream of a world in which only the New could be marvellous and desirable'. [61] This is true. But Rietveld, unlike Van Doesburg, tempered his enthusiasm for the New and the technological with the manual understanding of the craftsman. [62] The Schröder house, for all its references to the machine age, has many elements of the hand-made about it, particularly in the fitted interior and built-in furniture. Rietveld never indulged the technological determinism and rationalised futurism of other members of the De Stijl group like Oud and Van Doesburg; nor did he adhere to the philosophical dogmatism and absolutism of Mondrian. [63] Where Van Doesburg upheld the collective and preached the dangers of individualism, for Rietveld the individual was of foremost importance. He believed that the well designed artefact or building was capable of making individuals more aware of themselves and the space they occupied, thus making them also aware of their environment, and open to collective experience.

Photographs of Rietveld show a man whose hands were like those of a carpenter rather than a draughtsman. As long as the scale remained comprehensible when his ideas were enlarged into constructed or built form, their manual origin remained apparent. For such manual intuition cannot survive too great an enlargement (as with Henry Moore's over-inflated sculpture of later years). It was the 'small things' [64] which Rietveld designed that, like the Red Blue chair and the Schröder house, retain this quality: the

Summer house Verrijn-Stuart, on the Loosdrechtse Plassen, Breukelerveen, 1941

Zig-Zag chairs of the 1930s; some of the summer houses and weekend houses of that decade and particularly the Huis aan de Loosdrechtse Plassen, built on a river island in 1941 with barge-boarded walls and a thatched roof; the structure designed for parking bicycles in Utrecht of 1953 in which the jointing of the wooden structure is reminiscent of the Red Blue chair; the Netherlands pavilion for the Venice Biennale of 1954; the Sonsbeek Pavilion at Arnhem; the Steltman chair which Rietveld designed in the last years of his life. These share with the Red Blue chair and the Schröder house the intimacy and sensitivity of scale, that suggest prototypes not of a milleniary utopianism, but of life as it could be lived in the 20th century, a confrontation of the new and old, of machine and hand, wood and metal, brick and concrete.

At a time of critical and popular reaction against modernism, Rietveld's best work demonstrates that it is possible to design on a human scale without recourse to historicist ornament or a revival of Arts and Crafts practices and that simple standarized forms can be used with imagination and manual intuition. The opening of the Schröder house to the public with its interior restored to show the original arrangement of space conceived by Rietveld and Mrs Schröder in 1924-25 occurs at a time when architects and designers are more preoccupied with signs, symbolism and meaning in architecture than with concepts of space. But space was not the only concern of the designers of the house; consciously or unconsciously they also wished to embody modernity, individuality, sociality and choice as part of the meaning of the transformable space of the interior. Today we may have rejected, or regard as quaint, the notions of 'modernity' constructed in the designs and artefacts of the 1920s, but we nonetheless cannot escape being 'modern' — of our own time; and the individuality, sociality and choice inscribed in the interior of the Schröder house are as much issues of our time as they were of the 1920s. The Schröder house is both a 'monument of modernism' — a work of its own time, and a text which can converse with us today about our own conceptions of 'modernity', our ideals of living and the kind of spaces and sign-systems which we wish to inhabit.

Rietveld beside the maquette of a 'core house', 1929-58; design not executed

LENNEKE BÜLLER, FRANK DEN OUDSTEN

# Interview with Truus Schröder

The Rietveld Schröder House is inextricably associated with the life of Truus Schröder-Schräder; not only did she co-design the house with Gerrit Rietveld, she also lived in it for more than sixty years, looked after its material state, used it as a means to spread Rietveld's ideas and work, and provided the opportunity that we can all now enjoy of visiting this once private house.

When Truus Schröder died in April 1985, the house entered a new phase. With its restoration the Rietveld Schröder House changed its nature; it changed from a private home reflecting the patina from over sixty years of Truus Schröder's life, into the public space of a museum. The reconstruction of the 1925 situation may be seen as a first appropriation by the outside world, as an interpretation, an abstraction.

For these reasons, the interview published here occupies a central place in this book; it is a human document, which came into being on the eve of a new chapter in the history of the Rietveld Schröder House; it is a final report from a world that has passed.

In this interview, Truus Schröder presents *her* version of the Rietveld Schröder House, she reflects on Rietveld, she describes the essence of her daily life. For her, that meant living in a house that not only, as it were, took up a defiant stand towards the outside world and became an icon of modern architecture, but also, inside, revealed all the characteristics of a 'total interior', the sort of environment which led Nancy Troy in her Mondrian lecture in 1985, to pose the telling question: Paradise or prison? [1] What Mrs Schröder tells here is her own story, subjective and imprecise, but on the other hand direct, to the point, clearly reflecting the kind of person she was: full of life, full of enthusiasm, full of the ability to appreciate.

In 1911 Truus Schräder married Frits Schröder, a lawyer eleven years older than herself. The marriage proved to be a confrontation of two worlds, full of conflicting ideas about status, independence, the upbringing of children. [2] Partly to reduce the tension in their marriage, they decided to alter a room in their house in Biltstraat, and plan it according to the wishes, ideas and needs of Truus Schröder. Her chief requirement was to be able to withdraw into her own sphere, away from the conservative, lawyers' milieu her husband inhabited. She needed a room of her own, where she knew she could be herself and develop untrammelled.

It was in connection with this room that Truus Schröder and Gerrit Rietveld had their first real encounters. Rietveld was commissioned to alter the room. This meeting represented for them both a point of recognition, and was the start of an exceptionally fruitful collaboration, of mutual influence and exchange of ideas, that was to last their whole lives.

After the death of her husband, Truus Schröder's life changed dramatically. The need to live on a smaller scale, but above all, differently, led to the design and building of the Rietveld Schröder House in 1924. Whatever one may think of the house, at the beginning it represented for both Rietveld and Schröder the focal point of their energy, an explosion of creativity that solidified into the building with which we are now familiar.

**Mrs Schröder in the 1950s**

Rietveld once described what Truus Schröder meant to him, as follows: 'You strew the world with ideas; they say I'm a man with many ideas, but you have far more. I sweep them up around you. And they're not just any old ideas: they have direction. You are not the slightest bit interested in how something is to be achieved. You shouldn't try to be either. We must go on working as a team.'[3] What Gerrit Rietveld meant for Truus Schröder, emerges from this interview.

Mrs Schröder lived the majority of her life in the Rietveld Schröder House, and during those years she was confronted by a dilemma: on the one hand, she wanted to study and develop her personality in a stimulating environment, on the other hand there was the promotion of Rietveld's work, in which she staked her own conviction at the cost of her privacy. That history also forms a kind of monument.

In 1982, on 12 and 14 May, we recorded this interview with Truus Schröder. She had been rather hesitant to do this, largely because she was by then 92 years old. She had doubts about the accuracy with which she could recall her life in the Schröder house and with Rietveld, and wondered whether she could still put things in the right perspective. But it was precisely the manner in which, in a series of preliminary talks, she had told about her life that made us so eager to record this interview. Her openness and the way in which, even after 58 years, she still appreciated and enjoyed her home, constantly seeing new aspects and being able to present them in a new light — this was precisely what we wanted to record, an authenticity that we wanted to preserve. We realized that on many points this story would resemble the already well-known history of the Rietveld Schröder House. But there would be one essential difference: this would be Truus Schröder's story, reflecting her view of life, her experiences; including all those trivial, everyday events which historical accounts so often fail to record.

In order to reduce the noise from the motorway that skirts the Rietveld Schröder House, we decided to record the interview in the evening, with the first-floor sliding partitions closed around us to act as sound insulation. It is those talks, in edited form, that you can now read. Edited, because it was Truus Schröder's express wish that only a succinct form of the interview be published. We have done this to the best of our ability, both as regards content and form. Our criterion when we edited the interview was whether a particular passage seemed an authentic record of Mrs Schröder's views and her way of expressing herself. We hoped that the interview in this book would act as a personal guided tour through the history and the architecture of the Rietveld Schröder House. It should emphasize that the restoration of the building has altered something essential in the reality of the house; that the history of the Rietveld Schröder House has entered a new phase.

1. Nancy J. Troy, The totally harmonious interior: paradise or prison? *Piet Mondrian lecture* for the Sikkensprijs Foundation, *1985*

2. In a letter dated 1914, F.A.C.Schröder described his wife and the difference in attitude to life, between the two of them as follows:
'I take life as it comes, have a practical approach, and try to adapt it to my way of thinking. Your sense of right and wrong is determined by your reading, by your intrinsic self, and your life is shaped by these theories. You give precedence to that which most suits yourself, your nature and feelings. Herein lies, I believe, the essential difference between us; this is what makes you more theoretical and me more practical; you are more concerned with the spiritual, I with the material. You do not perceive society as it really is; you see society in its essence, how it ought to be. The differences manifest themselves in all our interests.'
Corrie Nagtegaal, *Tr.Schröder-Schräder, Bewoonster van het Rietveld Schröderhuis*, Utrecht 1987

3. Corrie Nagtegaal, 1987, op.cit.

**Mrs Schröder and Gerrit Rietveld in the 1950s**

Mrs Schröder and her husband, c.1911

The Schröder-Schräder family c.1920. From l. to r.: Marjan, Han, F.A.C. Schröder, Binnert and Mrs Schröder

*How did you first meet Rietveld?*
I was engaged to be married, and one day my fiancé asked me if I'd like to come round that evening because a new desk was being delivered. It was Rietveld who brought the desk.[4]
The desk was like they all were in those days, good workmanship, but very ornate. Not the kind of thing *I* was looking for in life. What I preferred was a certain sobriety, like you found in Berlage's work.[5] No, I didn't like that desk and I couldn't say I found it attractive.
Still, it wasn't Rietveld's taste either. Perhaps he had to make the desk — he worked in his father's business in those days — but it wasn't what he liked either. On that first meeting I think we both felt that the relationship was not that of salesman and client. But that's how it remained on that first occasion.
After that Rietveld would sometimes come to our house to repair furniture. On his own or with his farther. Then he set up business on his own,[6] and I lost touch with him for a while.

The house where we lived in Biltstraat was delightful, but I didn't like the proportions of the rooms. They were too high, that is, too high in relation to their length and width. I couldn't feel at ease in them. So my husband suggested that I have one of the rooms redesigned to my own taste. I think he made this suggestion because he felt that in many ways I was unhappy in our life together, that my interests lay elsewhere. But neither of us knew who to ask to redesign the room.
It was Cornelis Begeer, whom my husband knew in a legal connection, who came up with Rietveld's name. Rietveld had designed several things for Begeer and one day he asked Rietveld to design the jewelery shop in Kalverstraat,[7] and asked my husband if he'd like to come and see the maquette. My husband asked me to come along, because maybe Rietveld would turn out to be the architect I was looking for.
So I went along too. The design appealed to me greatly. I don't think my husband liked it so much, but he didn't have such an understanding of that sort of thing. I did think that the jewels — valuable objects — were too low down, too close to the pavement. It shouldn't be done like that, but otherwise I thought it was a good design. So when my husband asked me who I would choose as architect, I answered, 'I think I'd like Rietveld'. That's how we came to ask Rietveld to redesign my room.
It was a beautiful room, really beautiful, all different hues and shades of grey.
I remember my sister saying — she didn't visit very often, because she and my husband didn't get on too well together — 'But you never told me about this, that you've got such a beautiful room'. She was really taken with it. And Jacob Bendien had to come, he absolutely had to see it, because he was such a specialist in greys! Rietveld occasionally brought people to see it as well. That Berlin 'crystal architect' — I can't recall his name at the moment — came once and he liked it very much. Then there was Piet Elling, he came too.[8]
But of course the family thought: well, now, if your husband lets you

Number 135, Biltstraat, Utrecht. Mrs Schröder's room after it had
been redesigned by Rietveld, 1921

4. The first meeting with Gerrit Thomas
Rietveld (1888-1964) was in 1911, the
year in which Truus Schräder (1889-
1985) married F.A.C.Schröder.

5. H.P.Berlage, Dutch architect. Berlage
was one of the early pioneers of modern
architecture. His design for the Stock
Exchange on Damrak in Amsterdam
(1898-1903) was a major impetus for
the development of Dutch architecture.

6. In May 1917 Rietveld opened his own
furniture-making shop on Adriaan van
Ostadelaan in Utrecht.

7. Besides being a furniture designer,
Rietveld worked from 1919 onwards as
freelance architect; he was commissioned by Cornelis Begeer to rebuild his
jewelery shop in Oudkerkhof, Utrecht. In
1920 he received the commission to
rebuild the shop belonging to the Goldsmiths and Silversmiths Company in
Amsterdam.

8. Jacob Bendien, a Dutch painter, lived
in the same house as the Harrensteins
(Truus' sister An and husband) on Wete-
ringschans in Amsterdam (see Overy,
p.22).
The 'crystal-architect' was the German
architect Bruno Taut.
P.J.Elling, Dutch architect. Rietveld met
Elling in 1919 at an exhibition of the
painter Bart van der Leck at 'Voor de
Kunst' in Utrecht. Elling was one of the
few people who bought Rietveld
furniture in the early 1920s.

Rietveld — seated on the first version of the Red Blue chair — in front of his furniture-making shop on Adriaan van Ostadelaan, c.1918

Goldsmiths and Silversmiths Company, Amsterdam, 1920-22

decorate one of the rooms ... fancy making a room like that: not a trace of luxury, not a trace of wealth. Of course that was really absurd and incomprehensible! Nowadays I don't pour such scorn on these attitudes, but these people really thought something was missing.

*Did you know what sort of interior you wanted? Did you have a clear picture in mind when you were thinking who could design the room for you?*
Yes, I knew what I wanted, and it appealed to Rietveld straight away. Only, he added to my ideas, he took them further.
Rietveld saw exactly what I meant about the rooms being too high, he understood the problems I had with this. Whenever Rietveld made designs for rooms or interiors he indicated the height and showed how the furniture was to fit. In those days hardly any designer did that. It was as if the height was not significant. But Rietveld always created a harmony from length, breadth and height. For example, in a given space he would look for a multiple of three, for measurements that had a certain relationship with each other. Possibly he didn't do this so consciously in the Biltstraat house as in his later work. I can't really remember now.

*Had you seen the Red Blue chair [9] of Rietveld's — he had made it already, hadn't he, when he started redesigning your room?*
When he'd finished the room, Rietveld said, 'Now I'd like to put a couple of my chairs here'. He didn't want to sell them or anything, he just liked the idea of their being in that room.
We did put a couple of his chairs there, but I don't think there was the Red Blue one. I didn't like them though. For some time I found Rietveld's chairs quite a problem.

The Van Doesburgs and Schwitterses, during the 'Dada-campaign',
The Hague, 1923

*Tell us what it was like in the 1920s. Were you part of a group that was
interested in new ideas?*

I hardly met any people who had a feeling for what was modern. Not
through my husband. My husband was eleven years my senior; he had a very
busy practice and a great many acquaintances, some of his family lived in
Utrecht, and they weren't at all interested in that sort of thing. It was only
through my sister that ideas came in from the outside. We would discuss
such things in my room, and then it was mine, only mine. And once or twice
Rietveld visited me.

I wasn't interested in the world of my husband, but it was there just the
same. For better, for worse, I had adapted myself. I thought it ought to be
possible, I said to myself: things will change with time. But nothing changed.
Before we were married I thought we would be open to modern ideas: my
husband said that he didn't want any children and that I could study. Before
that, I'd only met young men who wanted to start a family, and that's not
what I was looking for. So I was never very keen, and then suddenly, this
man! A very handsome man. Extremely charming, and extremely annoying.
Only of course I didn't know that then. But really extremely charming and …
I fell for that. And I still understand why. He was very handsome, very tall
and broad. Yes.

But after my husband died things began to change. For example, Rietveld
came one time and asked if Kurt Schwitters could come one evening and
give a performance; Schwitters was in Utrecht for a short time.[10] So he
came. It was great fun, Rietveld had invited several people. I don't think I'd
asked anyone.

I remember very clearly how the children sat at the top of the staircase with
the maid, listening to Schwitters' booming. My goodness, could he boom!
And later when I went up to see them, the children told me they'd loved it,
but the maid said it was 'more than shocking'!

9. See Overy, note 43

10. German artist Kurt Schwitters
visited the Netherlands in January 1923,
for the 'Dada veldtocht' (Dada-tour). He
gave a series of Dada performances,
together with Theo and Nelly van
Doesburg. As well as this tour,
Schwitters also made some appearances
in private houses. On this particular
occasion at Mrs Schröder's he probably
declaimed Dadaist poems like 'Ursonate'
and 'Anna Blume'.

*What did you think of that 'Dada evening'?*
Oh, what was it Schwitters said to me? Something like, 'Habe ich Ihnen Freude gemacht'. I said, 'Yes!' — I'd really enjoyed it enormously. He made me laugh uproariously. Well, Schwitters liked that, he liked to 'entertain' you.

*In an article in 1929, Van Doesburg summed up the origins, aims and principles of the De Stijl movement. He wrote: 'We wanted to replace the brown world with a white one'.[11] What do you think he meant?*
Well, you see, all that old-fashioned stuff was brown. Everything was brown. Quite clear, really. I think he meant the world as it then was, it was 'grubby', it was not primal. I think all the people involved with De Stijl felt very attracted by this; find out the elements of which something is composed, analyze it, and then re-compose it. And of course you can't do that with brown. Take brown and you get nowhere. I think he meant something like that.

*When you and Rietveld began planning this house, did you have that feeling as well, that you wanted to replace the brown world with a white one? Was your aim in this way to build a modern house?*
It wasn't that I was determined to make something 'modern'. That was the direction I preferred. It was a spontaneous choice. I certainly didn't go to Rietveld with the idea of building some really startling house, not at all. But I knew what he'd made of that room of mine in Biltstraat, so I was

Two pictures of the Red Blue chair
Left: the first version, c.1918, as published in the *De Stijl* magazine in 1919
Right: a later version, c.1922, photographed in the Rietveld Schröder House in 1987. In the background is the Military table

11. Theo van Doesburg — pseudonym of Christiaan Emile Marie Küpper — published the article Der Kampf um den neuen Stil (The struggle for a new style) in *Die Neue Schweizer Rundschau*, 1929. The quotation referred to occurs in the following passage:
'The standard by which to measure a work of art was: how much did it yearn for the new. We wanted to replace the brown world with a white one. In these two colour concepts lay the deepest difference between the old and the new. The brown world found (...) its expression in the lyrical, the vague, the sentimental. The white world began with Cézanne, and led via Van Gogh and the heights of cubism, to elemental construction, to architectonic, unsentimental art. (...)
Arising out of this collective need for clarity, certainty, and regularity, I founded the magazine *De Stijl*.'

Above: end wall of the block of four houses on Prins Hendriklaan that the Rietveld Schröder House was attached to, 1924
Right: the situation in 1987, view of the southwest and southeast facades

convinced he was the person to help me.

I planned to stay in Utrecht for six more years [12] and then move to Amsterdam where my sister lived and where I had often felt very happy. So I wasn't thinking of buying or building a house. I wanted to rent a house where we could make some alterations. And Rietveld would be the one to make these changes.

But he didn't find a house, and neither did I. So he said, 'You'll have to build a house'. But I answered, 'No, I don't want to. I don't want to stay here in Utrecht'. He replied quite simply, 'Well, then you sell it again'. Yes, he was right about that. At a certain moment I decided that's how it would have to be. Let's go and find a plot of land.

One weekend we both went looking, he one way, I another. And when we saw each other again after the weekend, we'd both found a plot. The same one, this one. There was nothing else. My goodness, that was a crazy piece of ground, unimaginably ugly. A really filthy bit of land.

*I'd like to read you a short passage from an interview with Rietveld that was recorded here in the Rietveld Schröder House in 1963:*
'No-one had ever looked at this little lane before this house was built here. There was a dirty crumbling wall with weeds growing in front of it. Over there was a small farm. It was a very rural spot, and this sort of fitted in. It was a deserted place, where anyone who wanted to pee just did it against this wall. It was a real piece of no-man's-land. And we said, "Yes, this is just right, let's build it here". And we took this plot of ground and made it into a place with a reality of its own. It didn't matter what it was, so long as something was there, something clear. And that's what it became. And that's always been my main aim: to give to a yet unformed space, a certain meaning.' [13]
Yes, good ... it was really lovely, indescribably lovely. Too lovely to be true.

*So you and Rietveld decided to build a house on that plot; did you already have a picture of what kind of house it should be?*
If you gave Rietveld half a chance, he'd always start straight away. On this occasion too, he had a house ready, in a manner of speaking, the next day. [14] It was a delightful design, but I hardly looked at it, because it wasn't how I wanted it at all. Apparently, I had my own ideas about it, because what I wanted was in fact *this;* Rietveld too, though in another way.

The house he'd designed was very pleasant, but it just didn't appeal to me. In fact, I think it was more attractive than I realized; I know I scarcely looked at it. I must have been completely absorbed by something different.

There was an occasion when I'd baby-minded for a friend of mine who lived in one large empty attic room. I sat there that evening and imagined what it would be like to live somewhere like that. I think that was the beginning for me of thinking about this sort of life style.

*And what happened next?*
Rietveld made a sketch of the plot we could build on, and the question then was: what now?

I didn't give Rietveld a contract. People always say I did, but in fact he never

12. While her three children were still of school-going age and had all their friends there, Mrs Schröder wanted to remain in Utrecht.

13. Interview filmed by P.van Moock, 1963. The quotation referred to comes after the following passage:
'It is not a question of beauty or a certain theory of aesthetics, it is a matter of comprehension. If you comprehend something, it becomes real, and for me reality is what counts, not beauty or suchlike. I never consider whether something is beautiful or ugly. Beautiful or ugly are matters of highly personal taste. (...) That's all very relative. The point is, is a thing real, does it speak to you clearly. Then it's reality, then it's something. And that's what it's all about. For example, the space that had always been here, had not yet been defined. No-one had ever looked at this little lane, before this house was built here.'

14. Schröder refers to the 'preliminary sketch' of the Rietveld Schröder House. On this sketch Rietveld wrote beside the facade on Prins Hendriklaan: 'extension living room as scaffolding with glass'. In an interview with G.A.van de Groenekan (see Overy, note 31) it was recorded that Rietveld was highly taken with the image of scaffolding poles, bound with rope.
According to Van de Groenekan, Rietveld said: 'That scaffolding is so beautiful. When it's removed there will be nothing left. It will be terrible, because then you'll see those houses (...). Rietveld once told me it was such scaffolding that first suggested to him the idea of the intersecting wooden rails of the Red Blue chair.' (Interview with Lenneke Büller and Frank den Oudsten, 14 June 1982.)

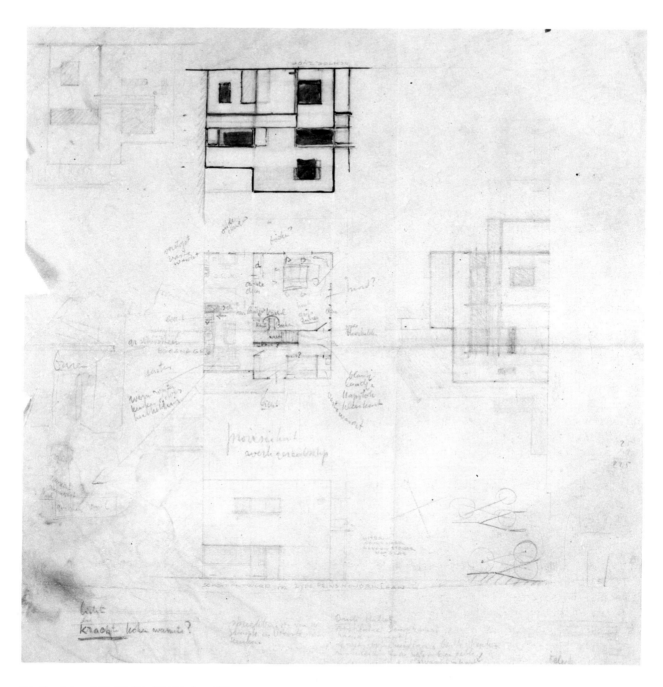

Rietveld; preliminary sketch of the Rietveld Schröder House, 1924

Rietveld; first sketch of the Rietveld Schröder House, 1924

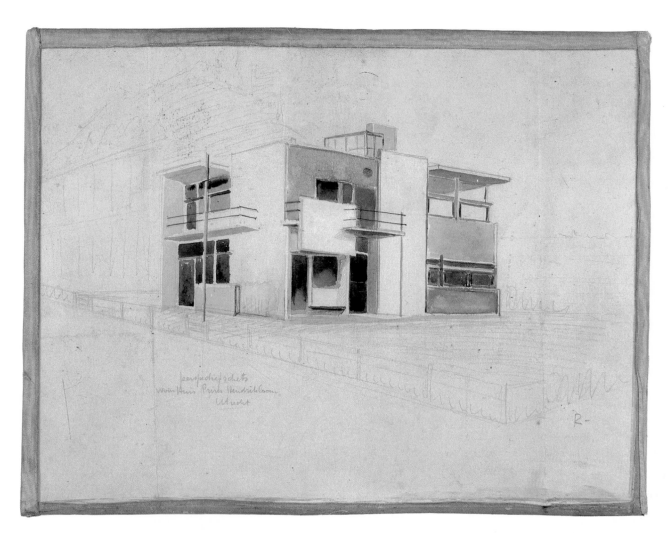

Rietveld; first maquette and second sketch of the Rietveld Schröder House, 1924

had a contract. Rietveld always made this clear himself. It was obvious from the start that we'd do this thing together. Still, you can't stop people getting it wrong.

We began, of course, with the plan. Usually people would start with the exterior — that's one way, of course — but we found it essential to begin with the plan. And to ask, what's the best view, where does the sun rise. That's how it all began.[15]

*If as you say there was no question of there being a contract, did the two of you see this as a chance to carry out an architectural experiment together?*

We never talked about it like that.

*It just happened?*

Yes, just as things were going along. We didn't make preliminary plans. As I said before, Rietveld made a sketch of the plot of land, showing the measurements. The next question was: how do you want to live?

Well, I was absolutely set against living downstairs. I've never lived this way, I found the idea very restricting. Rietveld was delighted about this, particularly because of the magnificent view.

So we started to map out the upper floor, because you can't do without bedrooms. A room for the two girls and a room for the boy — in fact, that's how we started, with 'rooms'. And where should we put them? All of us together, of course; the children had missed so much.

You see, I'd left my husband on three occasions because I disagreed with him so strongly about the children's upbringing. Each time, they were looked after by a housemaid, but still I thought it was horrible for them. And after my husband died and I had full custody of the children, I thought a lot about how we should live together.

So when Rietveld had made a sketch of the rooms, I asked, 'Can those walls go too?' To which he answered, 'With pleasure, away with those walls!' I can still hear myself asking, can those walls go, and that's how we ended up with the one large space.

But I was still looking for the possibility of also dividing up that space. That could be done with sliding partitions. I think that was an idea of Rietveld's, though he found it a shame. He did it, but he thought it was a pity. Personally, I'm eternally thankful that it was done.

*Why did Rietveld think it a pity? Did he think sliding partitions were not a fundamental solution?*

He always regretted it, primarily I think because the space upstairs became considerably more complicated with the placing of the partitions. You see, it was like having your cake and eating it: yes and no. And Rietveld would have preferred: it's either like this or like that.

In his own house he had one large area. Against one of the walls he'd made rooms for his children by placing partitions at right angles to the wall. Shut off with curtains, I believe. I didn't find this at all attractive, nor did I think it would be very nice for the children.[16]

15. See Overy, note 5

16. The interior referred to here is the third floor above the Vreeburg Cinema in Utrecht (designed by Rietveld and Mrs Schröder) where Rietveld lived with his family from 1939-58.
This third floor was described on the official plan as an attic. It was one large space, measuring 12 x 7 metres, in which Rietveld built a simple wc, a shower, a kitchen and a small bedroom for the parents. Opposite the side wall of the kitchen he constructed a row of beds for the children, which could be curtained off. (Frits Bless, 1982, op.cit.)

17. J.G.Wattjes, 1925, op.cit. He wrote as follows:
'The house designed by architect Rietveld on Prins Hendriklaan is an example of constructivist architecture. Not only in the exterior, but also in the whole interior planning of the house, new ideas have been pursued, while the application of colour is extremely unusual. The best way to give you an idea of what I mean is probably to draw your attention to a plain black ceiling with primary colours used for the rest of the room. The paintwork has not yet been completed, so no conclusion can be drawn as to the final effect. For the time being, however, my first impression of the interior colour is very satisfying. By rejecting the normal method of dividing space — with fixed walls — and choosing a system of sliding partitions, an extremely flexible arrangement of the interior is achieved. The whole upstairs can be used as one large space, with the stairs coming up in the middle; however, it is also possible to divide it up into a separate entrance hall and a number of smaller or larger rooms. The intention behind this "machine for living in" is not that now and again you can change the arrangement of the interior; it is that each day you can alter it several times, as often as your changing needs require. The question is, will such extreme flexibility in fact prove convenient in the long run; I very much doubt it.'

*In 1925 the architectural critic Wattjes wrote an article on this house, in which he wondered whether the sliding partitions would prove practical in the long run?[17]*

Not as far as sound is concerned, but otherwise, completely adequate.
Of course, it could have been shut off much more effectively, but Rietveld was absolutely against tampering with the floor or ceiling: they should be one unbroken whole. This has an enormous effect on the space. That's what we decided on.
Otherwise, a highly complicated structure would have been required, and Rietveld didn't want that at all. And I agreed with him, but the fact is, it makes your home so prone to disturbance by noise that it can be rather a nuisance. No, as far as the sliding partitions are concerned, once you know how they work, they're excellent.

*You and Rietveld agreed that the interior design and furnishings should form a unity?*

Yes of course. For example, the single chair I'd brought with me because I was rather fond of it, soon disappeared.

*So the house was furnished with entirely new furniture, specially designed by Rietveld?*

Yes. And while we were living here, that china cupboard was made. I don't think all of this was designed beforehand. The lift too, for example, that was designed and made later on. We were actually living here, and so we found out what we needed.
We moved in long before the house was ready; it was still terribly damp, and there was a heater and the work-bench here upstairs. Sometimes at night we shivered from the damp and cold. Then we went and sat close by the heater. I really was in the thick of it all!

*The living areas are situated around the stairwell. Did that idea stem from the interior of your house in Biltstraat?*

I never considered the house in Biltstraat as a blueprint. But I did know how delightful it was to have light falling from above the stairs — it made the landing so cheerful.
But you're right, in the house in Biltstraat five of the six rooms clustered round the stairwell were accessible through each other. That was very rare in those days. I believe that's one of the reasons why that house so appealed to me. And three of the rooms faced onto the garden — that was beautiful.

*You used a lot of glass in the upper floor. Such large windows were surely most unusual in those days?*

Yes, and I found it quite daring too, because in Biltstraat I had lived in a very 'protected' house. Then I came here, with all these huge windows. At first I had to have a form of shutter in front of all the windows at night. It was certainly most unusual, very odd and absurd. It was an enormous step to take, and I think it was only after another generation that people had got used to the idea of such large windows.

Ground floor, 1987
Left: the half-landing in the hall with the bench next to the telephone shelf. The door on the left leads to the studio, the door right
leads to the staircase
Above: kitchen with the Zig-Zag chairs from 1934. At the right by the
window is the shelf for the deliveries and shopping. In the background the glass noise barrier for the motorway can be seen

18. Interview filmed by P.van Moock, 1963. The passage referred to comes from the following:
'... the chair reffered to as the Red Blue chair — you know, that chair made from two planks and several rails of wood — was made to show that you can even make something beautiful, an object that has a powerful plastic effect, from completely straight, machine-made elements.
So I had some rails and one large plank sawn; then I sawed the large plank through the middle so that I had the seat and the back; and with the various-lengthed strips I then assembled the chair.
When I made that chair, I never thought it would turn out so important, both for myself, and possibly for other people, and I never anticipated that it would influence architecture in general. And when I got the chance to make a house based on the same principles as that chair, I seized it eagerly.'

*What one notices about this house is that for the period when it was built, much of the material used was also very unusual. Take the type of central heating — it's more like industrial heating.*
Well, it is. We thought central heating systems with vertical radiators were very ugly. Very much in the decorative style, it was all curly metalwork at that time. Rietveld liked what we've got here very much; he chose it. The only thing we didn't know, was that it would be so expensive. It turned out to be very complicated to install.

*We haven't yet talked about the ground floor. Didn't the original design also contain a garage?*
Yes, I thought then that everyone would at some point have a car, and it used to look very odd if you left that contraption parked in the street. In fact, I wanted the house to offer all sorts of possibilities. I didn't want to be dogmatic about what any part should be used for. I wanted to have it so that you could live in every room. And that's how we tried to make it: running water and electric points in each room, so that you could cook there if you wanted. Especially downstairs. And the idea of a garage fitted in with this.

**Plan of the ground floor. Drawing by Bertus Mulder, 1987**

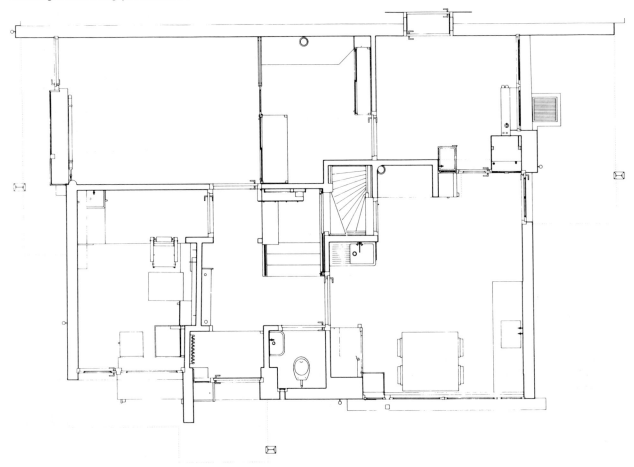

60

*In the small downstairs 'study' the light has been recessed into the ceiling, but in the hall beside it the same kind of light projects from the ceiling. Can you tell us about this?*

In that small room there shouldn't be any reflected light onto the ceiling; it is black, it is a 'hole', that's why the light's recessed. The ceiling is virtually 'non-existent', it should recede, making the room much higher.

I think that was brilliant of Rietveld, that little room, where you never have a closed-in feeling, even though it's so small. And one of the reasons for that is the ceiling.

In the hall beside the room, the light shines onto the ceiling, that's something different. And besides, the colour scheme of that ceiling relates to the colour scheme of the floor and the half-landing. And it's interesting as well that the downstairs ceiling is carried through almost everywhere, even though there are separate rooms; so you have individual rooms, but you see the ceiling extending beyond their walls. That was Rietveld's idea of preserving the perception of the total space. The only point where it's really enclosed is where we had planned the garage. The plan conflicted with the building regulations, at least I think that was the reason. But the kitchen, the room for the household help, the hall, wc and that small room are visually linked.

---

*Rietveld once said: '... when I got the chance to make a house based on the same principles as that (Red Blue — ed.) chair, I seized it eagerly.'* [18]

Good gracious, I didn't know that. How lovely.

You know, once I said to that chair: you came before the house, you belong in the house ... and ... you are the house! They are so closely interrelated. But I didn't know he'd said that. The chair isn't particularly striking here, at least I don't think it is. The house and the chair are one. It belongs here. And so the house must have been generated from the chair. But how exactly, well, don't ask me!

*The Red Blue chair and the Rietveld Schröder House are always associated with De Stijl, of which Rietveld had been a member since 1919. Was it in fact your aim to create a house based on the concepts of De Stijl?* [19]

Personally, I was not the slightest bit interested in De Stijl, it left me cold. I did like the fact that those people had new ideas, but that wasn't what I was concerned with. I wasn't interested in De Stijl, I was interested in Rietveld! In him as a person, in his personal vision. He admired De Stijl, but that didn't bother me.

I did want to know what was going on, because once when I visited Berlin I went into the 'Sturm' shop to buy a book. [20] Wasn't that a bit like the De Stijl movement?

And once I heard Van Doesburg give a lecture. Most interesting. I was very eager to hear and know about everything, but apart from that I didn't feel a great urge, a need to get closer. Yes, and once I was in a house that Van 't Hoff built in Huis ter Heide. [21] Actually that was not as extreme as this

19. In the magazine *De Stijl*, a new all-embracing idea of art was propagated, that would include existing art forms, without any one form losing its individuality. The ideal was to realize this new art in the everyday environment; in practice De Stijl attempted to create a new unity from painting and architecture.

20. *Der Sturm*: a gallery and magazine run by Herwarth Walden at Potsdamerstrasse in Berlin. Also refers to the circle of artists associated with the gallery and the magazine.

21. Architect Robert van 't Hoff built — between 1914 and 1919 — several villas in the village of Huis ter Heide, near Utrecht. Shortly before, he had spent some time in America, where he came in contact with Frank Lloyd Wright and his work. Schröder is probably here referring to the 'Summer house J.N.Verloop', for which Rietveld made some furniture. There is a draft letter dated 1959, from Rietveld to the German historian Udo Kultermann, in which he writes:
'I was commissioned to make furniture for a new house. My client showed me a book and said: "The architect based his design on pictures in this book." Then he asked me to make furniture in this style. (...) I made a table with chairs, but I didn't know what a distinguished designer I was following.
Van 't Hoff, who saw the furniture later on, came to my place and saw the Red Blue chair and the Buffet, both of which were unsellable. He invited me to become a member of De Stijl, which was then one and a half years old. (...) I became very good friends with Van 't Hoff and later on I saw more illustrations of Frank Lloyd Wright's work.'
The American architect Frank Lloyd Wright had an unmistakeable influence on the development of both furniture and architecture in Europe. *De Stijl*, I, no.4, 1918, pp.62-65, illustrated a work by Wright — The Robie House, Chicago, 1906 — with an accompanying article by J.J.P.Oud.

Left: ground floor, 1987; kitchen. The door on the left leads to the room for the household help, to the right of that is the service lift. The door with the blue shutter leads outside. In the foreground the Military chair, 1923

Above: first floor, 1987; view of Mrs Schröder's bedroom, the china cupboard and the service lift that connects with the ground-floor kitchen. The door leads to the balcony on the northeast facade

house is. It appealed to me immediately, but not so that I would have liked to make it like that myself. No, not like that.

The way Rietveld worked with height, well, that's the trick ... I don't know if the other De Stijl people were so interested in that ... but the relationship between length, breadth and in particular, height; that was something that really spoke to me. Rietveld's work is characterized by its proportions.

Also, when we began this house, there were no built examples of De Stijl-architecture. Maybe you could call the consulting-room Rietveld designed for Dr Hartog a 'Stijl-room' with its desk and chair constructed from wooden rails.[22] I never actually saw the room, but the photograph doesn't inspire me at all, although it was pleasant and looked fresh and new.

*But then, what did you and Rietveld think about the ideas of De Stijl?*
I never made a special study of the ideas of De Stijl. I hardly know what they are. And Rietveld? He didn't agree with them completely, nor did he disagree, in the beginning. No, certainly not.

You see, it was a group of very different people and if you start something new, then you can all assume for a while that you have the same goals, that you belong together. But gradually the differences emerge, they develop, then you grow more and more apart. Even at first, Rietveld didn't agree entirely. I don't know if he said so, because he thought it provided an important breakthrough. Really very good. But after those beginnings they all went their various ways, I believe.[23]

De Stijl was actually a very small group. It only gained more support later on. After that came the more practically-minded people: Functionalism,[24] a movement Rietveld also, for a while, wanted to feel at home in. But it soon became clear that Functionalism, too, had a different meaning for him.

*I'd like to ask you about an essential part of the design, the use of colour.*
That is entirely Rietveld.

*Within the De Stijl movement, cooperation between painter and architect, and the concept of 'colour in architecture', were central. Was there ever a discussion about whether the realization of this house — in the De Stijl manner — should be a combined project between painter and architect?*[25]
I understood various De Stijl members thought that it would be a joint project.[26] I don't know if they were annoyed with Rietveld about this, but it would never have occurred to me to involve those other people. I really wanted Rietveld to do it, because I knew what he was capable of.

No, it was such a specific choice for me. I would simply have refused to allow anyone else to work on it.

Rietveld didn't want to have a painter called in, and nor did I. As far as I was concerned, Rietveld was completely capable, so why call in a painter. Furthermore, I realized that to do so would make it turn out differently, and that it would be far more effective if we used Rietveld's colour conception. If a painter were to do it exactly like Rietveld, then you wouldn't have needed him. If he did it differently, then you ran the risk of getting a different kind of space: neither of us wanted to take that risk.

22. In 1922, Dr A.M.Hartog commissioned Rietveld to design his consulting room in Maarssen. Hartog, like Rietveld, was a member of the society 'Voor de Kunst' in Utrecht. This interior was Rietveld's first total design; besides black, white and grey, he used primary colours for the furniture.

23. Shortly after the founding of the group, differences of opinion about how to realize their ideal, both theoretically and practically, caused some of the founding members of De Stijl to leave. Although Rietveld always retained a certain distance, he remained a member of De Stijl to the end, probably because he valued both its existence, and the impetus it gave to the development of modern art and design during the 1920s. What could be described as the 'De Stijl concept' was largely developed and represented by Theo van Doesburg and Piet Mondrian. Mondrian's 'Nieuwe Beelding' (Neo-Plasticism) was, both in an aesthetic and an ethical sense, the theoretical foundation for De Stijl, particularly in the early years. Van Doesburg was the movement's driving force; his boundless energy and propaganda brought De Stijl international recognition.

24. Functionalism: international movement in architecture, c.1925-40. Its aim was to achieve the most rational solution for architectural problems, by means of thorough analysis: the architectural form should emerge from the functional solution of the requirements of the commission (Form follows Function)
In the Netherlands, Functionalism was chiefly represented by two architectural movements: 'De Opbouw' in Rotterdam (1920) and 'De 8' in Amsterdam (1927). Following the first CIAM Congress in 1928 in La Sarraz, De 8 and De Opbouw decided to work together. In 1932 they issued the first number of the magazine *De 8 en Opbouw*.

25. In its early years, various members of De Stijl, both painters and architects, worked together on projects, often of an experimental nature. These aimed to achieve a common goal: the establishment of a new, all-embracing idea of art in people's everyday environment.
Rietveld was also involved in several of these joint projects but only as furniture designer. He was never involved as architect in a joint De Stijl-venture.

26. When Theo van Doesburg, for example, heard Rietveld was working on the design for the Rietveld Schröder House (March 1924), he sounded out the possibilities of cooperation, witness this postcard:
'Dear Rietveld,
I hear from various quarters that you're hard at work. And I haven't heard from you myself for a long time. Apparently you've got an ideal commission ... is that so? Send me some news! As soon as you have some photographs, send me a few!
I suppose you'll do the COLOUR yourself. I haven't heard anything from you on that score! (...)
Write soon, signed with Does' Paw.'
According to Mrs Schröder, Bart van der Leck also proposed working together with Rietveld on the house. However, Rietveld rejected this idea of a joint project because of a fundamental difference in outlook about the use of colour in architecture.

First floor, 1987; view of the boy's room, seen from the living-dining area. Extreme left, the speaking tube that connects with the ground-floor kitchen; beside this the Stacking cabinet. In the foreground the End table

First floor, 1987
Above: looking through the house from the balcony on the northeast
facade. Left, by the window, the shelf for the telephone; beside that
the black cupboard for the washbasin
Right: view from the girl's room, with sliding partitions closed, so
that the first floor is divided into two, along the southwest-
norhteast axis (see plan). Left, Mrs Schröder's bedroom, then the
stairwell/landing, and on the straircase railings the small ladder
leading to the trap door in the skylight. In the foreground the Berlin
chair

First floor, 1987
Left: view of the boy's room, seen from the girl's room. Beyond the open panel of the sliding partition is the Stacking cabinet in the living-dining area. The glass doors lead to the balcony on the southeast facade. In the foreground the 'Chair constructed on tubular steel frame' from c.1928
Above: view from the boy's room, with the sliding partitions closed, so that the first floor is divided into two, along the southeast-northwest axis (see plan)

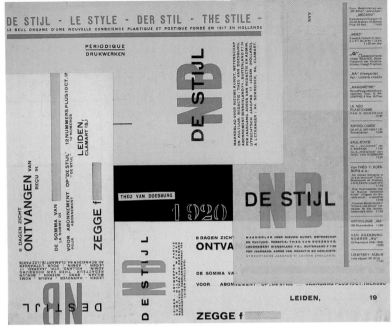

Left: Van Doesburg; collage of printing work for De Stijl, 1920.

Right: Van Doesburg and Van Eesteren; axonometric drawing of Maison Particulière, 1923

*In 1918, the painter Bart van der Leck published an article in De Stijl pleading for equal partnership between painting and architecture, based on separate, individual tasks for painter and architect. Put briefly, Van der Leck proposed that architect and painter neither can nor should assume each other's tasks. This would always be at the expense of one or other of the art forms, and at the cost of the purity of art in general. The architect, he says, should stop attempting to apply colour schemes in buildings, and should limit himself to his own profession. This was a prerequisite for the birth of a new modern architecture.*[27]

I cannot understand why colour should not belong to the architect's domain. After all, everything an architect uses already has a colour. It's impossible to avoid this, so why leave it all to chance? Then you can make conscious choices, then you can emphasize lots of things. A black wall is completely different from one in shining yellow!

*Van der Leck — I use his words — proposed, in contrast to the closed, contructive nature of architecture, the composing, deconstructive nature of the painter's art. What did 'colour in architecture' mean for Rietveld?* Rietveld thought that for a painter, a wall had a different significance from what it had for an architect. For an architect, a wall is seen as a spatial limitation, while a painter makes use of the wall for his ... well ... 'representation' ... whatever or however, but not as a limitation of space.[28] Later, I saw what Van der Leck had done in that flat in Vijzelstraat in Amsterdam — horrible, most off-putting; he used a wall as surface for his 'painting'. I didn't think that was a wall any longer.[29]

As far as I'm concerned, I agree entirely with Rietveld: it shouldn't be like that.

27. Van der Leck, Over schilderen en bouwen (On painting and architecture), *De Stijl*, I, No.4, 1918, pp.59-60. When the De Stijl movement was begun in 1917, Van der Leck had the most pronounced views on the use of colour in architecture. His views were the result of several — for him disappointing — cooperative projects with Berlage, in which painting always played second fiddle to architecture. In 1917, Van der Leck had more experience in this connection than any of the other members of De Stijl.

*But for example, take the colour design for the original floor here upstairs.*[30]

Yes, the floor, I think that's the real question. Did he perhaps overdo it with the colours there? I don't know. I've never solved that one.

There used to be a wide white stripe, near the stairwell. And when the children came home from school, I would call, 'Look out, the floor's clean'. Then they'd have to jump over the white part, because otherwise it was always getting grubby. And I didn't like having to say that. That was something I really disliked. The children told me later that they didn't mind at all. They thought it was quite fun, floors that you had to jump over. I thought it was educationally wrong.

Personally, that floor posed a lot of problems for me. The table stood on grey felt, on the edge of, or just overlapping, the white. And the Berlin chair was placed half on grey and half on white. Things like that really bothered me, because I felt they ought to stand on their exact spot. It really tired me out, finding them in the wrong position over and over again.

Rietveld made that floor when I was away. The house was all ready except for the floor. It all took so long, I said, 'You know what, I'll just go for a holiday to Switzerland and when I return, I hope the floor will be finished'. And when I came back, he had made this. I wasn't very happy with it, and I never could become happy with it. I found it too busy, much too busy. Rietveld did like it, but he altered it in the end. Perhaps because he found

28. Van der Leck, De plaats van het moderne schilderen in de architektuur (The place of modern painting in architecture). *De Stijl*, I, No.1, 1917, pp.8-9. We know of no texts by Rietveld from his De Stijl period which discuss the use of colour in architecture. The quotation here is from 1962, when Rietveld gave a lecture to mark 'Kleurendag' (Colourday) in Amsterdam.
'The painter's medium is colour; the architect's medium is space. If the architect uses colour, he does so to serve space. (...)
He (the architect, ed.) requires surfaces, as does the painter, but he needs them to limit space in such a way that they reflect the incident light, thus making the space visible, and making the light visible as a result of its reflection by the materials used. (...)
It may be that the most suitable material cannot be obtained in any other colour than one that is either too light or too dark as a reflecting surface. In that case it will have to be painted in order to produce the desired reflection.
There are various reasons that make the use of colour desirable or necessary. (...) A floor can be given a strong colour, for practical reasons, although this is undesirable because of light reflection. Then other colours are sometimes necessary on the walls to produce a balance. It is a question of what this space requires to make it as real and tangible as possible.
Sometimes the various architectural elements combine in the construction, to form a pattern, a rhythm, that is too insistent. Then you need to give them different emphases or use different colours. The kind of colour becomes secondary.
If everything is composed in greys, then each shade of grey can be made into a colour with the same degree of light reflection. We frequently see that the contrast of light and dark can be decreased when the colour contrast is as it were complementary. This seems to me the best application of colour in architecture.'

29. Mrs Schröder means the colour design for the apartment of Dr C.H. van der Leeuw in the Carlton building in Amsterdam. Elling, the architect, designed the interior of this apartment in 1949-50, and Van der Leck the use of colour.

30. During the 1986-87 restoration, the original colour design for the upstairs floor was re-created. In the photographs taken of the interior in 1981 it can be seen that the floor had been radically altered in the course of time.

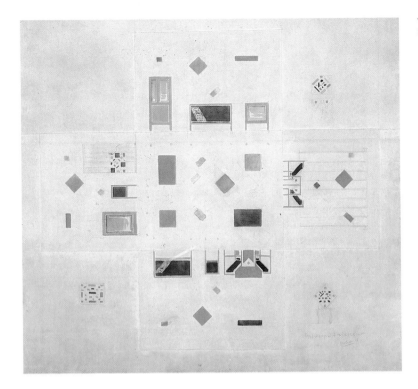

Van der Leck; interior design for a room in the house D'Leewrik, in Laren, 1918

Van Doesburg; colour design for a room in the house De Ligt in Katwijk, with furniture made by Rietveld, 1919

31. The Rietveld Schröder House occupies a unique place in Rietveld's work as a whole. It is not only his first complete building, but also the only architectural work, in which the vocabulary of De Stijl is extensively employed. After his experience with the Schröder house, Rietveld's interests shifted. His main preoccupations were with space and light. These came to determine the value of architecture for him.

32. Filmed interview by P.van Moock, 1963

he couldn't justify it, but it could be that he did it just for me. I've forgotten now.

But Rietveld said to me once that he sometimes wondered if he hadn't gone too far with colour. It was something that he pondered over — am I being like a painter now or ...[31]

I don't know really. It was certainly very light and cheerful. But I didn't have it under my control any more, it was too much for me. And I didn't think it was so beautiful as to outweigh its drawbacks.

First floor of the Rietveld Schröder House; presentation drawing by Han Schröder, made on behalf of the De Stijl exhibition of 1951 held in the Stedelijk Museum Amsterdam and the New York Museum of Modern Art

---

*What you wanted in the design of this house and your ideas about a life style, created several difficulties. Rietveld wrote about your ideas on this subject as follows:*

*'We didn't bother ourselves about adapting to the traditional houses in Prins Hendriklaan; we just placed this house here, and in fact, the strong contrast with its surroundings was just what we wanted. We didn't avoid older styles because they were ugly, or because we couldn't reproduce them, but because our own times demanded their own form, I mean, their own manifestation. It was of course extremely difficult to achieve all this in spite of the building regulations and that's why the interior of the downstairs part of the house is somewhat traditional, I mean with fixed walls. But upstairs we simply called it an "attic" and that's where we actually made the house we wanted.'[32]*

Yes, people sometimes say that the downstairs is plain conservative. People don't always realize that there was no alternative. For example, I wanted to have a wc upstairs, but the building regulations state that it must have a hallway around it. By labelling it an 'attic' we could make this large open space. So this was the attic, and that was accepted. Or perhaps some official thought: what's the difference anyway?

And Rietveld had drawn the house as if there were a pitched roof. Not because he secretly planned to have such a roof, but simply to suggest it ... the flat surface in contrast to the sloping one, they shouldn't notice that too much. So he softened the blow a little. Very clever.

*The modern movement architects of the 1920s saw this house as an important point in the development of architecture.*

*For example, in the writings of the architect Walter Gropius and Jean Badovici — publisher of the French magazine 'L'Architecture Vivante' — it is striking that they describe this house as if it were built from concrete.[33] Not surprising perhaps, since the use of new building materials and techniques corresponded with modernist ideas. Why was this house not in fact built of concrete?*

I don't think there were any drawings for the use of concrete. Rietveld had hoped it could be made of concrete. He wanted to build it with large concrete slabs, but at that time concrete was very new. I think that it was only made on the site, and you couldn't yet transport it, there was no way of doing that. It was an impossible job then, and would certainly have proved highly expensive.

33. Walter Gropius, German architect, founder of the Bauhaus in Weimar (1919), published *Internationale Architektur* in 1925, the first in the series *Bauhausbücher.* Here Gropius captioned a photograph of the Rietveld Schröder House: 'House in Utrecht: concrete, iron, glass'.

In his article, Entretiens sur l'architecture vivante, (Discussions on modern architecture), in the autumn number of *L'Architecture Vivante*, 1925, the French architecture critic Jean Badovici made the following editorial comment on the Rietveld Schröder House:

'This house is a practical application of the most recent ideas of the De Stijl artists, who have done all in their power to create a truly modern art form in the northern countries. Here you see, materialized and perfected, the ideas that the founder of the movement, Theo van Doesburg, developed in his article, "L'évolution de l'architecture moderne en Hollande".

The construction is entirely of iron, reinforced concrete, and glass. The plan avoids every form of symmetry and any a priori concept. The materials and construction involved are restricted to a minimum, while the plastic qualities of the house are absolutely clear and pure, as well as ingenious and original. The movable walls that run on rails make it possible to divide the interior into various rooms, as desired. The little furniture there is, is inspired by the furnishings of railway couchettes.'

First floor, 1987; left in the photograph, the boy's room, then the
girls' room, the stairwell/landing and the skylight.
The door in the girls' room leads to the balcony on the southwest
facade. In the foreground, the Hanging lamp.

East corner with the windows open, 1987
Left above: seen from the footpath past the house
Left below: seen from the balcony on the northeast facade
Below: seen from the living-dining area

However, the original conception was to use concrete, and then of course
it's a little odd that it was executed after all in brick. But also the house had
to cost as little as possible, no more than six thousand guilders.
Rietveld himself didn't find it 'wrong' that the final house was not made of
concrete. I thought it conflicted somewhat with his principles about being
true to the materials you used, but that was different for Rietveld. That
cupboard door, for instance, you say to yourself: that's made from something white. But it's painted white on one side, and on the other it's just
unprimed wood. You may interpret this as inconsistency, but you can also
see it as 'the most inexpensive solution'.

*The modern movement was very enthusiastic about this house, but how,
for example, did the neighbours react?*
They didn't like it. People stood and discussed it with each other. In the
weekends crowds would come to have a gawp. Did I never tell you that story
about a friend of mine? She was a very striking woman, tall and well-built,
and she stood here taking a good look. Beside her stood a fairly solid-
looking chap smoking a cigar. He clapped her on the shoulder and cried, 'But
my dear child, how can you possibly like that?!' In a tone of voice suggesting:
you can't be serious! That really appealed to me, these two beside each
other, and him saying, you surely can't be serious?
But that's the way it was. One person would defend the building, someone
else would tear it to bits. Quite a happening!
It wasn't so nice for the children. On one occasion my daughter Hanneke
came home from school quite scarlet in the face, crying her eyes out, so I
asked her what was the matter. She sobbed, 'I told a lie, because they said
to me, "You live in that loony house" and I said that I didn't live in that loony
house'. Something like that was very hard for a child to cope with. Oh dear
me yes.

Southwest facade, 1987

*Can you recall any personal reactions from members of De Stijl?*
No. Only I happened to find out what Oud thought.[34] Oud came to take a look, saw the sliding partitions, and laughed. Then he saw something else, and laughed. He laughed at everything. That really irritated me, because I didn't think that was the most significant aspect of this house, how practical it was or how amusing.
But there was also a young man on that visit; I met him once again years later. I don't remember now who it was, but he told me: 'Oud was really moved by what he saw here. You didn't notice that, but he was really shaken. I think it made quite an impression on him'. Rietveld and I hadn't noticed that at all.
Maybe deep down Rietveld and Oud were kind of rivals. I think Oud sometimes felt he was the father of modern Dutch architecture, when in fact he wasn't. He made some good things, but they belong to an earlier period. I think the real ... yes ... breakthrough, came from Rietveld, not Oud.

Oud wrote to Rietveld once saying that it harmed the development of modern architecture, that Rietveld's work was so lacking in solidity. That his architecture looked so shabby after a while, was so prone to wear and tear, that sort of thing. But Rietveld didn't take this to heart. He had his reasons for how he worked: if you didn't build things incredibly cheaply, then you simply didn't get the chance to build anything. Certainly not to try something daring. And it didn't have to be something you yourself thought was daring, but everyone else probably did.
No, that 'solidity' wasn't something Rietveld really cared for.
That fragility in his work ... no, fragility is the wrong word ... but making things in just such a way — an old-fashioned architect would say: 'Couldn't that have been more solid, more massive?' — but no, and that's the point, it shouldn't! That's why it's so beautiful. And it works!

34. J.J.P.Oud, co-founder of the De Stijl movement in 1917, Rotterdam city architect; left De Stijl in 1921, following a disagreement with Van Doesburg about the use of colour in Spangen, a housing estate in Rotterdam.

View of the southeast facade in 1963, when building on the raised motorway had just started. Extreme right in the photograph are the 'Row-houses' in Erasmuslaan designed by Rietveld and Mrs Schröder

You can look at it like that too.

No, that solid, massive stuff, Rietveld didn't want it at all. That's clear if you look at his chairs too, it was in fact a sort of ... liberation, that he wasn't bound by the need to produce something solid.

And Rietveld thought houses shouldn't last for too long. They grew old, and should be replaced by another type of space utilization. So they didn't have to be so durable. I think Rietveld was far more extreme than Oud in this way. I think it was an enormous difference between the two of them, this question of solidity; make things in just such a way ... don't try to build for eternity, or to last the centuries. If you think of this house, it's a bit contradictory, because a short while ago it needed to be thoroughly restored, and that proved very expensive.[35] But Rietveld never expected this house to last so long. He didn't think that was necessary or desirable.

You know, materials weren't what mattered most for Rietveld.

After all, an architect's real material is space[36] — that is completely incorporeal — and that was very important for him. What you did with space, indoors and out. The way space was defined had to be right, both inside and outside. In itself that's very complicated, but he managed it beautifuly here. That's why Rietveld was so enormously upset when they started building the motorway nearby. The entire physical setting with which he had interacted, was destroyed. Of course it was unpleasant for us to have the traffic there, but they just didn't see that the whole setting was turned topsy-turvy, irrevocably. They didn't understand how incredibly important the exterior of the house was in relation to its particular setting. Something I only realized myself after quite some time. I thought it was beautiful, but I didn't understand that it fitted so exactly in this spot, nor why that was.

And it was perfect, the way it was!

Sometimes, when I approached the house from the Rhijnauwen side,[37] it was as if I made inner contact with a canal house in Amsterdam. I felt it to be so strong, it stood there so secure. Of course you can also see it as a 'flimsy' structure, but at such moments I found it very firm. And that firmness is not something to do with solidity but with ... posture. The posture of the house in contrast with the street.

If I imagined what it would be like with a pavement in front of it, so that the house stood on an extension of Laan van Minsweerd, then I thought it was an attractive town house too. It was still a more or less detached house, but that wasn't uncommon at the outskirts of towns, and that's what it was rather like here.

Laan van Minsweerd was a very fine street. There were houses along one side and trees on the other. And you always asked yourself: why are those houses so beautiful? They were built in three colours, using three types of stone: grey, a shade of brown, and finally pink. And then across the road the green around the barracks. Pretty. It was always enjoyable to walk down that road. There were even flat roofs. I liked the idea of becoming part of that street; and that's what we really thought, that our house would be part of Laan van Minsweerd.[38]

35. The exterior and parts of the interior were restored in 1974. (See Mulder, pp.107-112).

36. Rietveld, Architectuur, *De Werkende Vrouw*, 1930, no.11-12:
'... this is the striking characteristic of all architecture: people live in it, on it, among it, around it. So I want to make one thing absolutely clear: whatever else architecture does, it must never spoil space. Architecture is what our space-sense experiences as reality.
The material used, the shape or the colour of pillar, wall, window frame or roof should never take first place. In architecture we are dealing with what is in between, within or beside the actual work. If this is a good place to live in, it is because of the quality of the space.'

37. Rhijnauwen lies some distance southeast of Utrecht.

38. In making the design, Rietveld and Mrs Schröder had assumed that Laan van Minsweerd would be extended, according to the 1920 city extensions plan for Utrecht by Berlage.

First floor, 1987; view of Mrs Schröder's bedroom-study, which is now — after the 1986-87 restoration — the reconstructed girls' room. On the chimney column a portrait of Rietveld from the 1960s

Mrs Schröder, portrait taken during the interview

L. to r.: Laan van Minsweerd c.1925, Sculpture Pavilion Sonsbeek,
Textile factory 'De Ploeg' and Van den Doel house
Right below: Netherlands Pavilion for the Venice Biennale

*The idea of building an entire street like this house, a larger complex, did Rietveld and you think of that?*
No. Rietveld never thought of this house as a 'model', you see. You have to understand that it was the luck of the draw, this spot. It was bordered by one wall only. We had the freedom to design outwards on three sides, that was absolutely marvellous. Conditions were optimal, because this is a corner house. What we did here would be impossible in a row of terrace houses. It really was the luck of the draw, but also, we both appreciated what we'd got, and made the very best of this setting.

——————

*How do you see this house in the context of Rietveld's other work?*
I think he came across a lot of practical questions here that were useful to him in his later work. But he always tried to make things simpler than he did in this house. He thought this place was too complicated.
He never thought this was his best house, you know. And if you asked him: what do you think is your best house, he didn't know. He once proffered hesitantly: 'Maybe Ilpendam'.[39] His client there was the easiest one he ever had to work for.
I think that in this house Rietveld isn't so completely 'Rietveld'. I think he adapted himself somewhat to what I wanted. And I believe I loved this house more than Rietveld did. There's so much of myself here, I respond to the whole atmosphere of the place. And I don't know Rietveld's other houses so well. I don't like his other houses as much, but then I'm prejudiced, of course.
What I find personally, is that he achieved more with his large buildings than with houses he built. You hear it said that Rietveld's large buildings aren't his best work, but I think that's nonsense. It was just that he was good at small buildings, but he could certainly make large buildings too, just think of what he made in Sonsbeek, Venice or the factory in Bergeyk[40] ... Oh yes, I think his large works are superb.
Rietveld had an enormous artistic sense — I think he was a truly great artist. The trouble was, he had to build houses, dwellings, all the time. And of course he enjoyed doing that; he said: 'So long as I have achieved something with each house; I don't just want to be out on the sidelines'.

39. House Van den Doel, in Ilpendam, 1958-59

40. Sculpture Pavilion Sonsbeek, Arnhem, 1954; subsequently rebuilt in the gardens of the Kröller-Müller Museum in Otterlo.
Netherlands Pavilion for the Venice Biennale, 1954.
Textile factory 'De Ploeg' in Bergeyk, 1956.

84

First floor, 1981; view of the living-dining area with Zig-Zag chairs (including the 1942 Armchair) photographed through the movable window on the staircase railings. In this photograph the movable shutters for the staircase railings are also closed. Right, the bookcase, part of the interior since 1936

**Rietveld in the 1960s**
**Rietveld's handwriting, from a sketchbook containing the speech he delivered on the occasion of his election as honorary member of the Dutch Architects' Association, 19 March 1964**

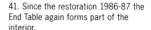

41. Since the restoration 1986-87 the End Table again forms part of the interior.

42. Mrs Schröder refers here to the philosophical theory underlying Mondrian's work. Mondrian's 'Nieuwe Beelding' (Neo-Plasticism) can be seen as a structuring principle that aims to create a dynamic balance between unequal but equivalent quantities. Mondrian based his idea on the order of the universe, the dynamic relationship between opposites: day and night, ebb and flood, male and female, internal and external, spirit and substance. Mondrian expressed this 'evolutionary principle' of the universe, of universal, cosmic relationship, in his paintings. His work is concerned with the expression of pure proportion: horizontal and vertical lines, planes of primary colour in different positions and sizes, are juxtaposed in a delicate balance.

43. Rietveld, manuscript, 4 January 1963:
'The complexity of all that exists is as unending as the immeasurability of the distance between the indescribably tiny and the unspeakably huge. The idea that only mankind is capable of self-knowledge is quite unjustified and without foundation, so that it would be better to assume that all evolving life — that is, as far as mankind is capable of comprehending in this connection — is a process of becoming more aware. In fact this remains completely imcomprehensible to us, although we partly experience its effect in our own lives.
The consequence of this assumption is, that we find ourselves in a totally democratic environment; and assuming for a moment that man as a conscious creature is the most developed being, then it follows that he should be most responsible for his attitude to life. (...) For centuries, viewed from the standpoint that man was superior to matter, the greatest virtues were considered to be so-called spiritualization, self-sacrifice, and compassion, while egoism was decried as the root of all evil. But backstage, as it were, self-preservation of necessity remained the driving force in human existence. Compassion soothed the conscience, and served to cover the deficiencies of our society. Why not openly acknowledge the conflict, that in essence we have the same nature as beasts of prey. We do not have the strength of a tree, which only borrows a little water and light, stands unprotected in harmony with its surroundings, furthermore providing shade and fruit. But we do know how to prune ourselves.
An architect is no revolutionary, is not qualified to prescribe rules for a simpler society. But in his own profession he can contribute something to this, that may even serve as an example in certain ways. The history of architecture reveals

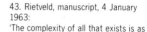

beautiful shapes and solids, monuments of confidence, of human power and presumption. But let us instead place the emphasis on space, and be as cautious as we can in constructing its limitations. Do not let our *joie de vivre* and enjoyment of all that we have, be dependent on bourgeois satisfaction with our houses and the perfection of our latest gadgets, but on a respect for the careful and economic manner in which the quality of space has been adapted to basic necessities. (...) Limitation does not mean impoverishment, on the contrary, it is the only and most human way to experience reality. Our senses bear witness to this, analyzing our susceptibility in terms of seeing, hearing, tasting; and then subdividing our seeing into perceiving shapes, colours and space, sub-dividing colour perception into red, yellow and blue; three sorts of sensitivity of the retina. Thus the nature of our powers of perception indicates the means which enables us to experience together the luxury of frugality.'

*What do you find typical of Rietveld's work?*
The dimensions; the interrelationship of the dimensions. That's what I find most characteristic. The dimensions were so subtly interdependent, that always moved me very much. For example, if Rietveld were renovating a room then he would search for measurements that could be combined with each other. Then he would suddenly say: 'I've got it'; and then all the jigsaw puzzle pieces would fit. But if, for example, the length and the width didn't fit in with the rest of the room, then he'd alter part of it, make part in a different colour, or something like that. And usually it turned out just right, turned out very beautiful.
And what else? I think his things are very straightforward and uncomplicated. Even when I think of his chairs, it's obvious that they should be the way they are. He would work at something until he had got rid of its superfluities. I think the Zig-Zag chair is a very fine example of that.
I don't think that 'form' was Rietveld's chief concern. The End table, for instance, he actually thought it was a mistake; he thought he'd taken things too far when he made it. Of course, it was once again a dissection of the construction of a table — that's probably how he meant it to be — but it became more of a thing, a sculpture.
I've just remembered something funny. A student came here once, and if you ask me he was really looking for something to criticize. Then his eye fell on that table where the leg stuck up, just a little, through the top. He thought that was naive! Well, what could I say? Was it naive? Yes! But why shouldn't it be naive? The whole thing was in fact naive. It was a funny little table. I havn't got it any more, I got rid of it. A pity, but it demanded your attention, it was so conspicuous. [41]

*The facade of the house on Prins Hendriklaan has sometimes been compared with a Mondrian painting. Was the work of Mondrian a source of inspiration for Rietveld?*
I don't know. I can only say what I think myself.
I had a visit once from a Mondrian connoisseur, and that man walked round here as if he had a slight toothache. Well, I can appreciate that, I thought, Mondrian gives me a slight ache too. Mondrian just doesn't go in this house; it's funny, but it's really impossible. The whole thing presents such a unity, and Mondrian just doesn't fit in. They're absolute opposites. Once I had a Mondrian reproduction hanging here, but it really didn't go. It had a completely other kind of life, a spiritual, abstract life. [42] With Rietveld it was completely different.
Rietveld experienced life through his senses, and that 'abstract' manner was nothing for him. The only thing of which you can be certain, is what you apprehend and can digest through your senses. That was your reality.
I found that of the essence, it spoke to me at the deepest level. I don't have the same refinement as Rietveld had in perceiving things through the senses — that didn't in fact interest me greatly — but I understood it very well and found it a reliable ... 'guide'.
Now, in Rietveld's scheme of things the 'Umwelt', the cosmos, was both very important and very great. In comparison he felt himself to be nothing but a tiny, insignificant speck. I don't know how Mondrian talked about such

Above: southwest facade, 1981
Above right: southwest facade seen by evening, 1987
Below right: Mondrian; 'Composition with red, yellow, blue and black', 1921

things, but when Rietveld started talking about the cosmos you became deeply impressed by the immensity of all that surrounds us. Nevertheless, he cherished his own insignificant place and did not try to go beyond it. But what he did do, he wanted to do responsibly, and well. [43]

*Did Rietveld talk about these subjects with you when you first got to know each other?*
I think he was very preoccupied with them already, but I don't think he could actually formulate these ideas.
When I first got to know Rietveld, he, like myself, had been through a lot of unpleasantness. We had a deep understanding of each other's problems with the social norms of our times, which were strongly present.
At that time, Rietveld really had to break free from the strict Protestant beliefs with which he had been brought up. And because I had just broken free from religious conventions myself, I think I, yes ... I think I encouraged this in him. So the ground was prepared, as it were, but I think that talking

First floor, c.1925; view of the living-dining area. Right, under the windowsill, is the sloping shelf where the Schröder children did their homework

with me helped him sort things out. For a while we were deeply involved with each other's problems and helped each other to develop further.

At that time Rietveld had hardly written anything. I really urged him to write things down. Later, he and I worked together,[44] but I was very interested in these things myself. With a piece of architecture, so many other questions are involved, I don't like that at all. But I didn't want to give up the other contact that we had and nor did Rietveld. He enjoyed talking with me. But sometimes, if I said, 'Yes, but Rietveld, if you put it like that people won't understand you', he would reply, 'Then it's not for them'. And then he wouldn't change it.

*Would that be typical of Rietveld, such a reaction?*
Yes. I remember for example that Charley Toorop[45] once said: 'Rietveld, you know those chairs of yours, I'm always banging my ankles on them'. To which Rietveld replied, 'Sorry about that Charley, but it's other people who deserve to give their ankles a good bang on those chairs, not you'. But with the implication: there are some people it would certainly be good for. Yes indeed!

*You not only worked on projects with Rietveld, you also had a very close friendship with him up until his death. What was it in his character that appealed to you?*

I was captivated by Rietveld's ideas, I loved his attitude to life. Everything he did was so solid. You might say, it was all so flimsy, but no, it was so meticulous. And for me that went together with Rietveld's idea that it was vital to experience reality through the senses. [46]

Yes, and his theory of 'sobriety', that appealed to me greatly. I needed that very badly, I wasn't a very sober person. But he was, and in two ways: there was something uncomplicated that was very characteristic of him, and then as well — what he also described in that speech he gave in Delft [47] — never to live in a way that harms something else. You can't actually avoid it, but try to do it as little as possible. That was a beautiful speech. Some people were really carried away by it, though of course there were others who thought it was overdone.

---

*I'd like to ask you about something quite different now, that we haven't discussed so far. How was the house to live in, in practice? When the house was fully complete, did you have the feeling that you'd created a good environment in which to live?*

I thought it was very good for the children to live in an atmosphere like that, also to have Rietveld often around. To have that experience. To hear those conversations, including those with people who disagreed. In fact, to take part in that exchange of ideas. I was very pleased that the children could share in that.

And for myself? Well, this house exudes a very strong sense of joy, of real joyousness. That's something in my nature, but here in this house it's stimulated. And that's absolutely a question of the proportions, and also of the light; the light in the house and the light outside. I find it very important that a house has an invigorating atmosphere; that it inspires and supports *joie de vivre*.

*Was the atmosphere stimulating for Rietveld?*

No I don't think it was, particularly: I think that we were still too preoccupied with petty details. I do think that he found me a stimulating person, but whether my milieu was stimulating for him, I couldn't say.

And he didn't really like all the admiration the house got; I mean, he wasn't particularly interested that it was so famous. Of course he was pleased that someone like Lissitzky admired it. [48] And also that it provided him with openings to do more. But it wouldn't be true to say that Rietveld really basked in the fame of the house.

*How did Rietveld like living in this house?*

He didn't live here very long; just at the end of his life. Then he said once: 'It's really quite a nice house'. But it was too complicated, according to him, especially with the sliding partitions. He didn't even know how they worked, and I'd gone and had them slightly altered as well. No, he didn't show what he thought of it.

44. See Overy, note 3

45. Charley Toorop, Dutch painter. In 1931 Rietveld designed the interior for her house in Bergen, Holland.

46. Rietveld, Inzicht (Insight), *i10*, December 1928, wrote:
'All that we experience results from the working of our senses. Our being perpetuates itself through sensory perception. (...)
The direct experience of reality, of the ordinary simple things that are right in front of us, for which we need only stretch out our hand, and open our eyes that direct way of experiencing life, is rarely found. Much of the restless discontent and dissatisfaction, especially among people who have all that is supposed to be necessary for a contented life, stems in fact from the need to experience reality directly. (...)
A painting by Picasso or Van der Leck is, in contrast with our daily chaotic and immediate sensory impressions — alongside the essential — in fact the ordinary direct reality, albeit expressed in colour.
Architecture can also bring us closer to reality. (...) Architecture should not be a slave to existing needs, it should also reveal primary needs. Architecture should not be the statement of space, but the intense experience of it. The reality that architecture can create is that of space.'

47. Short speech given by Rietveld on the occasion of receiving an honorary doctorate in the technical sciences, from Delft Technical University; 11 Jan. 1964.

48. El Lissitzky, Russian constructivist artist. In 1926, Lissitzky and his wife visited the Netherlands. Dutch architect Mart Stam showed them the Rietveld Schröder House. (See Overy, pp. 32, 33, 38).

Mrs Schröder's painting by Bart van der Leck; 'Composition '18-'21'

First floor, 1981; view of the living-dining area showing the 1963
Steltman chair

*Rietveld once said that you are the only person who could really live here. You've lived in this house for 58 years now; do you agree with that?*
Yes, I sort of think that's true. That you stick it out.
I've developed a more carefully thought-through attitude as a result of this. In spite of all my doubts, I think that deep down it's taught me a great deal. I'm looking on the bright side now, because of course you could just as easily say that I'd lost a lot of things, done a lot wrong. Because I did bite off more than I could chew. I mean, to live in a house like this, the way you think you ought to live in it. I often couldn't manage that. And I wanted to educate myself more, but I didn't do that either. I got sort of stuck here, although I do think that I did grow, progress somewhat because of this house.

*What has it meant to you to live in such a famous house?*
Living in it, what does one really see of it?
I often liked the fact — though again, often I didn't — showing people the house and watching their enthusiastic reactions. You know, I wanted to make propaganda with it — I had the idea that I could spread such ideas convincingly. Not by means of words or rhetoric, but by allowing people to see the house and experience it. People sometimes thought it odd that I always let visitors come, but I was always being asked. And I nearly always had the feeling that people carried something away with them — though of course, you never know how long that lasts.
I don't like it if people come to visit me completely unannounced. But I suppose the reason for that is that I suspect I don't live in the house the way I should: not fully enough, not tidy enough, not the way it ought to be, not the way such a house requires. But of course I can't always live in the style this house demands.
A delightful thing happened recently: some people visited me in connection with the future of this house. As they were leaving, one of them, a pleasant, older man, looked at that painting by Van der Leck[49] and said, 'Look at that Van der Leck there ... a fine work'. To which one of the others replied, 'Yes, and a fine mess underneath it'. 'Yes, but that's life', was my reaction, to which the first man assented, 'Yes, that's life'. So enthusiastically — as if to say, that's allowed! That really gave me a fillip. To accept the state of things as they are: a painting by Van der Leck and underneath, the mess of life. Nothing you can do about it.

I wanted a real exchange of ideas in this house. That was one of my aims. I wanted to have people here that you could discuss with. People with a critical attitude, all sorts of people. The criticism was less than I had expected, but what there was, was more tangible. Different from cultural evenings, when you come home bubbling with ideas, which have disappeared after a couple of days because you have moved on to the next subject. Actually the discussions here were always on the same topic. But in fact I liked it that way. Not so much a question of a famous house, but something to do with the essentials.

First floor, 1981; view of a working corner in the 'guest room' which is now — after the 1986-87 restoration — the reconstructed boy's room. On the left, the 1936 bookcase

49. In 1982, a painting by Bart van der Leck, *Composition '18-'21*, hung above a bookcase in Mrs Schröder's bedroom-study which is now, since the restoration of 1986-87, the reconstruction of the girls' room.

First floor, 1987; view of the living-dining area

Same view as previous page, with blinds closed

First floor, 1987; view of the skylight seen from the living-dining area

*What are those essentials?*
That someone feels really spoken to. That someone who comes here takes something away that he or she can ponder over, and maybe reconsider. I think that's what I mean. And I think that's what happens with most people who come here. Of course there are some who come just to 'to pick up the art', but on the whole not too many.

*What do you think will happen to the house when you aren't here any longer?*
The house was in fact designed for a family to live in, and of course it won't have that function any more. It will have a different purpose, I assume.
I wouldn't open the house to the public as it is at present, but that's for the foundation [50] to decide, and opinions differ on this point. You could reorganize it and ... suppose some young people were to come along and say, 'What an interesting chair, how's that chair constructed? Can I take it apart, can I hold it upside down? Can I take a look at it?' That sort of thing.

50. Rietveld Schröder House Foundation.
(See Overy, note 4)

First floor, 1987; view of the skylight seen from the stairwell/landing

And perhaps they could have the facilities — downstairs, or in a shed maybe — to try things out. I'd like that, things going on in the house. And of course that would attract a different type of person.

But agreement hasn't yet been reached about what to do with the house. Someone thinks it should be restored to its original state, and someone else says, 'No, it should be restored to how it was when you had lived in it for several years, but when the children were still with you'. But whatever happens, it will of course be a very different place.

What I should dislike is if someone were to come and live here who had a completely different philosophy of life — I don't mind if it's a better attitude than the one I have — but I mean someone who would say: that house will have to adapt to my wishes. Yes, I should really dislike that.

BERTUS MULDER

# The restoration of the Rietveld Schröder House

## THE ROLE OF MRS SCHRÖDER IN THE RESTORATION

Truus Schröder lived in the house at 50, Prins Hendriklaan for sixty years. Towards the end of her life, she took steps to ensure the maintenance and future of the house. In 1970, at the age of 81, she and her children initiated the Rietveld Schröder House Foundation which purchased the house from her and assumed responsibility for it. Mrs Schröder was one of the members of the foundation and for many years attended its meetings. After nearly fifty years the house needed many repairs, particularly the exterior; so one of the first tasks of the foundation was to make plans for its restoration. In addition, the future of the house had to be decided.

To prepare and oversee the restoration an architect was needed. Clearly, Mrs Schröder should select this architect. In August 1973 she visited me with her youngest daughter Han, who is also an architect, for a preliminary talk. Mrs Schröder knew that I had worked for Rietveld at the end of the 1950s, and that I had lived in his former apartment with my family, after he had moved to the Schröder house in 1958. She knew that Rietveld and I got on well together and that I'd helped him in various ways such as clearing out his apartment on Vreeburg square in Utrecht. We talked about Rietveld, the Schröder house, how to tackle its restoration, and about my own work. Finally she asked me for addresses of houses that I had designed myself, so that she could gain an impression of them. Shortly after this, I heard from the foundation that the restoration of the house would be entrusted to me. I felt this to be a very great honour, indeed felt almost burdened by the responsibility.

I needed to acquire a certain confidence before I began to restore so famous a house; to make a thorough study of its history and try to gather all available information about it. But information was difficult to obtain. There were hardly any drawings that corresponded to the house as actually built. Although Rietveld had made a large number of working drawings, in the realization of the house things had been done in a different way from the design these indicated. The alterations subsequently made had been executed without plans and carried out according to Rietveld's directions. So we began a survey of the house as it was while Mrs Schröder was still living in it, carrying out the minutest measurements. This revealed some remarkable facts. One thing I noticed was that the angle irons which served as balcony railing were attached to the steel I-beams in a strange manner. The obvious way of attaching an angle iron is to weld the flat side to the I-beam. However, that was not what had been done. The blacksmith had attached the angle irons by the front of the flat part. The surface that can be joined is thus very small, so the smith filled the space between the sides of the angle iron and the pillar, which looks very strange. Mrs Schröder told me that the smith had thought the best way to fix the angle irons was the opposite from the usual way, because he'd noticed that everything in the house was different from what you would expect. When Rietveld saw how it had been done, he let it be, because he didn't like having to change people's completed work.

The people who built the house sometimes put Rietveld to the test. For example, they fitted the strange asymmetrical window frames upside-down,

Southeast facade, 1987

to see if Rietveld would notice it was different from his drawing.
Not only did I make a survey of the house as it was, I also tried, through talks with Mrs Schröder, her children and people who had worked in the house, to develop a picture of its beginnings and history. I was helped in this by the 31 photographs, of excellent quality, taken in the first years, the glass negatives of which had been carefully preserved by Mrs Schröder in her archives. These photographs show clearly what the house looked like, how it was decorated and furnished in the early years, and also reveal Rietveld and Mrs Schröder's intentions in building the house. The photographs were taken for publication, so the camera angles were selected and the furnishings arranged to give a clear impression of their intentions. I was particularly helped by the many discussions I had with Mrs Schröder. She was always willing to talk about the house and had preserved in her memory an impressive mine of factual information. And always present in the background, although then dead for nine years, was Rietveld.
Mrs Schröder was also involved with her house in a very practical manner. There were a couple of places where the roof leaked when it rained and the wind blew from a certain direction. She kept a careful eye on these. If a few

drops leaked in, the water had to be caught in something to prevent further damage. She became very inventive about this sort of thing. Sometimes the sliding partitions came out of their rails. At a certain level of ground water the cellar would flood. Mrs Schröder greeted such events as if they were all part of the order of things. She knew that a house not only brings you happiness, it also does the opposite. When she grew older I took over this kind of job for her and this taught me a great deal about the house and some of its shortcomings.

Mrs Schröder always tried to present the house in such a way that it represented as clearly as possible both Rietveld's intentions as regards the space and the light inside and the carefully balanced 'total image' of the outside. That is why, for example, she had a room that had been built onto the roof, removed in 1958.

When visitors were expected — especially if they were people whom she thought might be influential for Rietveld's reputation — she got up early to tidy the house and to remove things that disturbed the sense of space inside it. She regretted that because the first floor was now used differently, all the original partitions could not be slid aside, and the entire open space could no longer be shown. It also bothered her that the interior had become somewhat shabby and had lost its former clarity. However, it was not possible to redecorate this while she was still living there.

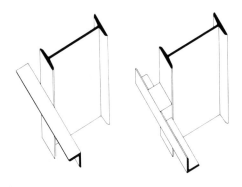

Way in which angle iron is attached to steel I-beam (left: the obvious way). Drawings by Bertus Mulder, 1987

When the roof room, added in 1935, was removed, the slender steel stairs that led to the room remained in the light well, leading up to the skylight in the roof. This meant that the way light fell from above on the upstairs interior was not the same as originally intended, when it was regulated by a trap door. Mrs Schröder would explain this when she showed people round the house, because she wanted them to be able to imagine how it had been originally.

She always found these visits quite exciting. When the people came upstairs, the partitions were pushed back. She would observe the visitors to see if, on coming upstairs they were struck by the space and light, or whether they rushed to the well-known points and immediately began to take photographs. That determined for her the nature and the length of the guided tour.

She didn't want the house to be kept just as she left it, because in the course of years the interior had been adapted to the life of a very old lady, and so its original sense of space had become obscured. She thought it would be good to restore the original conception of space, light and clarity, but she never stated explicitly how this should be achieved. She left that to the foundation to decide.

The exterior of the house was restored while Mrs Schröder was living in it. She was then 85 years old. Scaffolding was erected around the whole house, various windows and doors were renewed, the plaster and brickwork were repaired, and there was a large quantity of dust and dirt! None of this perturbed Mrs Schröder in the slightest. She was actively involved in all that was going on around her, convinced that it was all for the best for the house and would increase Rietveld's reputation. Never once did she complain. When the first stage of the restoration was completed, Mrs Schröder wrote

to me: 'I searched and waited a long time before I found the right man to whom I could entrust the restoration of this house. I do sincerely believe that I have made the right choice, and I am most appreciative of your dedication and involvement in the work of Rietveld.'
After reading this letter, my confidence was secure.

─────

## THE RESTORATION

Between 1974 and 1987, the house was restored in three stages. First the outside, in 1974; then the garden and fencing in 1983; finally, the inside was restored and partially reconstructed in 1986-87.

In the first stage, it was a question of thorough repairs to the exterior. Rietveld thought that a house should have a life expectancy of about fifty years: in his terms, this house, half a century old, had weathered very well. But now some of the consequences of certain technical shortcomings could no longer be ignored.

The walls, which Rietveld had first thought of making in concrete were constructed from brick, and plastered on both sides. The brickwork, together with the plaster, had cracked in various places, because some of the walls, which themselves had to carry beams and pillars supporting the roof, rested on steel beams which had bent under their heavy weight. Because the brickwork could not give, it had cracked. Other cracks in the brickwork and plaster were caused because iron embedded in them was not sufficiently protected against corrosion. Another possible contributing factor was the nearby explosion of a German ammunition lorry during the Second World War. The cracks needed repairing, because they allowed moisture to penetrate the wall, and this was detrimental to both paint and plaster. It appeared that in various places the plaster had worked loose, and so some walls had to be entirely replastered.

The balconies had been constructed from concrete. These are thin slabs internally reinforced with small steel beams that extend into the house and are attached to the wooden beams running through the floor. What had happened was that rain water had penetrated the concrete slabs, rusted the steel reinforcement, and caused cracks in the concrete. This needed alteration, because the process of corrosion was accelerated by further seepage through the cracks.

Furthermore, there had always been problems with the roof. With the materials available at the time of construction — asphalt paper, tar and lead — it proved virtually impossible to seal the point of juncture between the roof and the smooth and austere walls that rise above the roof level. What we did was to remove the entire roof and wall covering, replacing it with a seamless synthetic covering that runs over everything that sticks up above roof level, as far as the front edge of the walls. We have today finally reached a point where suitable materials and methods of construction have been developed for the forms that Rietveld conceived in 1924.

The design of the wooden exterior frames for the windows and doors was developed by Rietveld from the role that he assigned them visually in the total image of the house. They act as secondary elements, as a kind of

Page 108: detail of southwest facade, 1987; view of the vitrine-like extension of the studio. The photograph shows to a certain extent how the space between the angle iron — that serves as balcony railing — and the yellow I-beam, has been filled in the process of welding
Page 109: ground floor, 1987; view of the studio window. In the background the viaduct carrying the motorway across Prins Hendriklaan

Restoration of exterior, 1986

filling, necessary framework for the glass. So they are coloured black. Parts of the framework are worked into the walls. In other places the front surface of the exterior plaster, the window-frame and the window, all lie in one plane. This kind of detail mocks the building methods of 1924, based on craft traditions. However, on the whole these presented no problems, although after fifty years some parts, including the astonishingly large windows, had to be replaced.

After all the repairs had been completed, the paintwork was completely renewed. All previous coats were removed, and the entire outside was repainted. This proved the most challenging part of the restoration, because our research into the present state of the house had not clearly established the original colours. So out of sheer necessity I had to decide for myself exactly what colours to use. Black and white, very frequently used, were of course no problem. And I knew the red, yellow and blue that Rietveld was accustomed to use. Red tended towards vermilion, yellow to chrome, and blue was ultramarine. When we removed paint and found the early coats, this was substantiated. But it was more difficult to ascertain the exact tones of grey used on some of the walls — five shades between white and black — because these were not always mixed in the same way. The relationship between the tones remained the same, but in the type of paint applied and the actual tint, changes occurred through the years. When he built the house, Rietveld thought that he could achieve the various grey tints by adding colour to the plasterer's mortar. This is what he prescribed in the building specifications. However, it didn't work. I think in fact it would be difficult to obtain a harmonious effect in this way in conjunction with white-painted walls. Probably the walls were later covered with whitewash which had colour added to it for the grey or off-white surfaces. This also proved unsatisfactory, because it was very patchy. You can see this clearly in the old photographs. When the paint industry had developed casein emulsion paint suitable for exteriors, this was used, and looked much better. Later, synthetic emulsion paint was used.

Whenever the house got a fresh coat of paint, Rietveld would determine on the spot which tones of grey were to be used. He and the painter would mix the colour, apply a little, consider it from a distance, and come back to look when it had dried. If he was not satisfied, they tried again. One painter who did this with Rietveld told me that once he had to give the surface above the kitchen window seven different coats, before Rietveld was happy with the result. He was paid a bonus for his patience.

After Rietveld died, Mrs Schröder gave instructions when the house was to be painted. On the last occasion that this happened before the restoration she sent the painters away when they had scarcely begun because she could see that it was all going wrong. On each new occasion, Rietveld would make decisions about the tones of grey, and they were always slightly different. We made a study of the different coats of paint which had been applied one on top of each other, and I concluded that the variation in brightness between the tones became less in the course of time and that in the beginning the greys were mixed with ochre, while later they tended more towards blue.

Right: detail of southeast facade, 1987; view of the kitchen windows and the signs: 'Goods delivered here' and 'Ring first; if no answer, use speaking tube'

First I tried using standard greys from the paint manufacturer's catalogue. But when I had applied this paint, I saw immediately that this method was too unsubtle. I, too, would have to mix the colours on the spot, apply them and correct the tones until I had obtained a balanced total effect with black, white, red, yellow and blue. This had to be done on the spot because the effect created by the colour and its brightness are strongly determined by the light that falls on it, and strongly affected by the adjoining colours. I tried to mix greys that did not suggest a particular colour. The relationship of brightness between the tones is the same as in the early years, so that the overall impression is now more striking than in the years preceding the restoration.

Restoration of first floor, 1986

In 1983, thanks to a donation, we were able to begin the reconstruction work of the garden, paths and fences. This was the second stage of the restoration. The situation immediately around the house had changed and we had to make adaptations. In 1925, the site included a far larger piece of ground than today. An extra piece of land had been rented on the southeast side and a long fence with three gates in it along the Prins Hendriklaan side enclosed the property.[1] What we have now done is replace the fence along the border of the property belonging to the house and put a gate round the corner, opposite the main entrance.[2] This refers to the original urban plan to extend Laan van Minsweerd past the house, which induced Rietveld and Mrs Schröder to put the main entrance on this side. The road was in fact never extended although there is now a footpath running past the house here. We were able to reconstruct the fence, using old photographs of the exterior and a detailed drawing by Rietveld, now in the municipal archives. The ground around the house was raised to the same level as the pavement in Prins Hendriklaan, and then planted. Mrs Schröder was, considering her age, very active in this: she wanted flowers and shrubs which grew wild in that area. She wanted it to look natural, not too cultivated — no planned herbaceous borders.

The garage, which had been built after the war, had been placed on a lower level than the house, so as to attract as little attention as possible. This garage, situated behind the house, is now used for storage. The patios under the balconies, the three entrance gates, and the garage, are linked by concrete paths; two steps lead down to the garage. The concrete is not reinforced, will gradually crack, and then small plants will grow in these cracks. That was how it used to be. Rietveld would even speed the process on its way, by taking a hammer and making cracks in the concrete.

Before we started the reconstruction, the surroundings of the house looked like a no-man's-land. Once the fence was fixed, and the garden planted, the house regained its own setting, a clear territory, and Mrs Schröder felt this sense of regained privacy, so that when it was fine she would go and sit outside on the blue bench beside the front door.

The third stage was the restoration and reconstruction of the interior, and this took place after Mrs Schröder's death, in April 1985. We were able to begin straight away, because we had started preparations many years before. This also meant that there had been ample opportunity to discuss

1. see ill. pp.24-25

2. see ill. pp.6-7,50-51

3. see ill. pp.10,65,86-87,97

4. see dust cover and ill. p.67

with Mrs Schröder, and other members of the foundation, the way in which this stage of the restoration should be tackled. There had to be detailed discussion about this, since the interior, unlike the exterior, had been altered in the course of time. We had to decide whether to retain these alterations or return to the original.

It was finally decided to restore the interior in such a way that the use of space and the sense of space would give an idea of how it must have been in the first years after the house was built. The qualification was added that this did not mean reproducing exactly the original state. Those elements which had been determining factors in making the house a blueprint for a new style of living and a new approach to architecture as the art of designing space, and which had been subsequently lost through alteration, would be reconstructed.

The sense of space and the way in which space was used, are closely connected in the house. All the elements from which Rietveld composed this sense of space are formal responses to functional requirements proposed by Mrs Schröder. There are a wealth of examples: the three small wooden blocks with which the doors of the china cupboard in the living area can be opened, and which point in three directions at right angles to each other; the black, white and grey sliding partitions; the black surfaces behind the children's beds, which are made from board, because plaster would be too hard and cold here; the red, yellow, blue and black metal running tracks for the partitions along the ceiling; the dark painted surfaces in the kitchen in areas that get dirty quickly, and so forth.

In order to recapture the original sense of space, many of the original furnishings and functional apparatus of the house had to be restored or returned. Thus, for example, the sink unit and cupboard above it in the kitchen were built in again, and the service lift linking the kitchen and the living area was restored. Mrs Schröder's bedroom was furnished as it used to be, with a replica of the bed, a little shelf for the telephone, a small shelf for her watch and one wall partially painted in yellow. The kitchen, which had been built in that room in 1936, was removed and placed in the documentation centre. The place where the children had slept was newly furnished with copies of the original beds, washbasins, wall cupboards, wall coverings and so forth. In the living area, the work surfaces beside the table were renewed, and the reconstructed Stacking cabinet replaced the bookcase that had been built in 1936.[3]

The trap door controlling the light from the skylight was remade. The sliding partition system was restored to its original state; the number of possible space combinations had been reduced by the later changes introduced by Mrs Schröder. The large partition that separated the children's rooms had been halved in size because it was so difficult to slide — with the result that the partitions no longer extended to the staircase. It was then no longer possible to make one large area by combining the boy's room with the living room, or the girls' room with the stairwell/landing.[4] Copies of the original lamps were made upstairs. Throughout the house, with the exception of the entrance hall, new floor coverings were laid, corresponding to the originals, composed of grey and black felt, black and white rubber, red painted floor-boards, and grey, brown and yellow linoleum.

In the early years of the house, 24 black-and-white photographs had been taken of the interior, which were very useful in our reconstruction work. In order to gain a full picture of the former situation we had often discussed these photographs with Mrs Schröder and her children, and with Gerard van de Groenekan who, as a furniture-maker employed by Rietveld, worked for some time on the interior of the house.

However, we were not content to work on assumptions, we wanted to base the reconstructions on as much detailed, accurate evidence as possible. Many of our questions concerning measurements, materials, colours and how parts actually functioned, remained unanswered. But, we could still formulate these questions and we knew where to look in the house, behind or underneath fixtures or furniture which had been added later.

We began to remove part of the floor covering and plaster from the wall of the former kitchen, where the sink had been. We expected to find traces of the wooden frame to which the sink had been attached and the cupboard above it from which we could deduce the measurements we needed. We found what we were looking for, and this brought us a good step further. Later, we found lengths of wood under the cellar steps sawn ready for kindling; these were from the cupboard above the sink. We also found out that parts of the draining board had been used to make a working surface in the studio. Piecing all this information together, we were able to construct a new sink unit and cupboard. We re-made those parts we had found which proved incomplete.

We spent hours peering at the photos, trying to work out how the shelf in the kitchen on which to place deliveries and shopping had folded away.[5] Then like a ripe apple falling into our laps, came the answer: in the most obscure recess under the hall stairs, we found the original board. That's the way things happened.

We were able to work out the measurements of the wall cupboards in the girls' room, because we found the original fittings in the wall under the plaster. We found the water pipes and drains for the children's washbasins and the electric lights above them behind a wall covering that had been added later. When we removed the floor covering, red-painted sections of floor were revealed. We also found pencil lines and incisions, made when the floor covering had been cut, which were very useful when we came to determine the original floor pattern.[6] It was very exciting when we found traces of original parts which should have been there according to old photos. After carefully scratching or chipping away the outer layer, there they were.

We also made unexpected discoveries. For example, when the floorboards were taken up in order to fit the pipes for the washbasins, we found that the warm water pipes which ran under the floor, lay in a simple wooden casing filled with sawdust. Even in such a pracitcal matter, Rietveld was far ahead of his time. He came up with solutions to problems which were often later applied in industry.

We spent several more months' detective work inside the house; then the jigsaw puzzle was more or less complete. The carpenter could start his work.

5. see ill. pp.31,59

6. see ill. pp.74-75

7. see ill. p.27

Thorough restoration of the upstairs had to be made because some of the plaster on the walls and ceiling was cracked and loose. On the ground floor various small local operations sufficed.

The upstairs bath, dating from 1936, was not changed. The grand piano, formerly in the son's room, has not yet been returned there, largely because the Red Blue chair that was later brought into the house, can in fact only stand where the piano stood.[7]

After the brickwork had been repaired, safety devices installed, the electricity, plumbing and heating systems renewed, and plaster and woodwork completed, the whole inside of the house was painted. The colours of the wood and metalwork, which were black and white, red, yellow, blue and grey, were mixed according to the coats of paint that we had found in the house. However, we had to make a choice about the grey, because we found different shades of grey (although all of them were mixed with ochre), dating from different periods, in different parts in the house. We found no blue-grey mixtures inside.

Just as with the exterior it proved a complicated business to determine the exact colour for the interior walls. Beside black and white there were yellow, two shades of blue and three shades of grey, all of which had to be mixed. These greys were also mixed with ochre. The hall ceiling was lavender blue and was never repainted. So that was simple, and posed no problem. In the case of the yellow, we found traces of the original colour in Mrs Schröder's bedroom which had remained after the new kitchen was built there in 1936. The chimney column upstairs had first been painted in this shade of yellow, then in lavender blue like the hall ceiling, and later on several times in ultramarine. We experimented with the different colours in the same sequence, and concluded that the final colour of ultramarine, the strongest, was the best in combination with all the black and the powerful red.

Here, as with the outside, we had to experiment a great deal before we could determine the precise shades of grey: in fact, it proved even more difficult than it was outside, because the way the light fell on the different wall surfaces varied greatly.

When finally we found what seemed to be a good balance with the other colours of the interior, we discovered that this had far-reaching conse-quences for the combination of colours with which we had already painted the exterior of the house. On one of the walls in the girls' room where a grey section extends through to the outside, we found we had produced two different greys. So we decided to repaint the grey wall outside, but this upset the balance of the exterior colours; they appeared too blue in comparison with the greys inside. Thus all the greys outside had to be repainted.

This delicate adjusting of the interior and exterior greys to the different quantities of light and the different juxtapositions of colours absorbed me for many weeks and caused quite a few headaches. A coat of paint applied towards dusk on a cloudy day looked unexpectedly different the next morning, dry and in sunlight. It was fortunate that the painter I was working with took it as a matter of course that we continue until we achieved the result we wanted.

Cross-section southwest side
Above left: boy's room
Above right: girls' room
Below left: study. Below right: studio
Drawing by Bertus Mulder, 1987

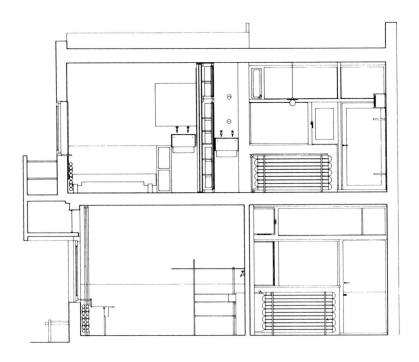

Cross-section of the side adjoining the next property
Above, l. to r.: girls' room, wc, bathroom, Mrs Schröder's bedroom
Below, l. to r.: studio, workroom, household help's room
N.B. The door in the household help's room was placed there during
the 1986-87 restoration and links the house with the documentation
centre in the adjoining property
Drawing by Bertus Mulder, 1987.

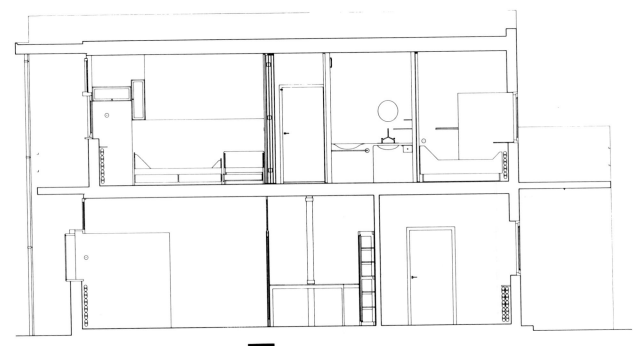

Cross-section southeast side
Above left: living-dining area
Above right: the boy's room
Below, l. to r.: kitchen, wc, main entrance, study
Drawing by Bertus Mulder, 1987

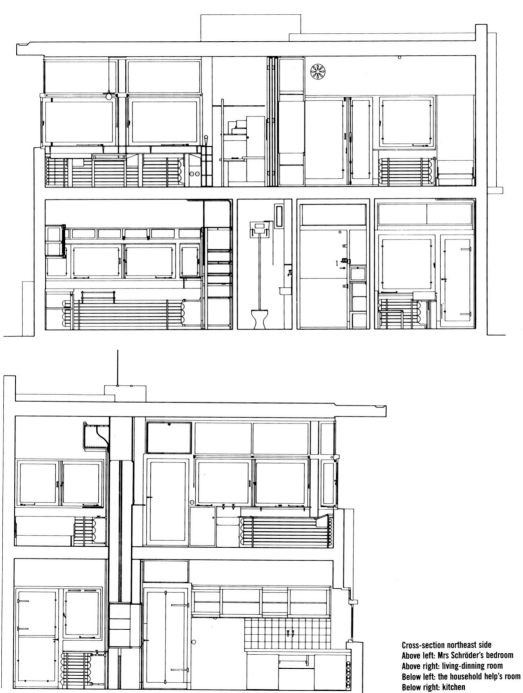

Cross-section northeast side
Above left: Mrs Schröder's bedroom
Above right: living-dinning room
Below left: the household help's room
Below right: kitchen
Drawing by Bertus Mulder, 1987

First floor, 1987; looking towards the girls' room with view of Prins
Hendriklaan. In this photograph the sliding partition that seperates
this room from the boy's room, is shut

First floor, 1987
Above: Military chair and End table, photographed in the girl's room
Below: looking into Mrs Schröder's bedroom, from the bathroom
The black cupboard for the washbasin is open

## THE SPATIAL STRUCTURE OF THE HOUSE

In 1944, Rietveld wrote in a reflection on art:
'Tagore says concerning art: "by limiting the illimitable, truth becomes reality." This is the simple reality, neither ennobled nor spiritualized, that the artist constructs for us as part of our awareness. Art is the clearest form of reality. The painter teaches us to experience reality by defining colours, the sculptor by defining materials, and the architect by defining space. Although in the architect's case the material and construction are essential, the space in, between, and around the solid form is of primary importance'.[8]

The principle governing the way in which Rietveld dealt with space and space-defining elements can be seen on a card that Rietveld made to thank everyone who had acknowledged his seventieth birthday. On this card he sketched three free-standing walls, based on the letter *R*, positioned in such a way in relation to each other, that they enclose space (inside) which can thus be distinguished from the remaining space (outside). In this system the walls function as partitions, and the openings between these walls as transitions between inside and outside. This, in a nutshell, is the grammar of Rietveld's architecture, which he worked out while designing the Schröder house, and which he consistently applied there. Undoubtedly this was because he was working in collaboration with Mrs Schröder. The same consistent application of this principle can later be seen in his Sonsbeek Pavilion in Arnhem.[9]
Although Rietveld had already made the Red Blue chair, the Berlin chair and the End table, he was not yet ready to apply these principles directly to architecture. Apparently he needed a 'warming-up period'. His first designs for the Schröder house, both the preliminary sketch and the first model[10] are still bound by the traditional concept of an enclosed inner space with incidental openings to the outside, completely dependent on the main mass: a box with holes in it.

Because neither Rietveld nor Mrs Schröder were happy with this, Rietveld continued to develop the design. Soon after, he made a sketch which shows a gigantic breakthrough in working with the idea of delimiting space.[11] Instead of a mass with holes, we now see a system of elements that determine space, using the same principle as the 'thank-you card' described above. This consists of a number of space-dividing elements, that determine unambiguously what is inside and what outside. In addition to these are transitional elements such as eaves, balconies, pillars, railings, door-frames and window-frames which relate to both inside and outside. These elements structure the transition between inside and outside in a different way in each situation, depending on the position and function of the space, and on the light.

The first sketch is still somewhat schematic, because the vertical separating elements that jut above the roof dominate, and the groups of transitional elements are enclosed by them. In the second sketch the horizontal elements are developed further, especially at the south corner, so that a

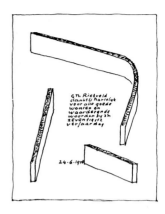

Rietveld; 'thank-you card' made on the occasion of his 70th birthday, 24 June 1958

8. Helma van Rens (ed.), 1979, op.cit.

9. see ill. p.84

10. see ill. pp.53,55

11. see ill. p.54

12. see ill. p.55

13. see ill. p.79

14. see ill. pp.108,109

15. see ill. pp.74-75,118

16. see ill. pp.6-7,105

17. see ill. p.14

18. see ill. p.31

19. see ill. pp.15,30

20. see ill. pp.6-7,68,105

21. see ill. pp.74-75

balanced three-dimensional whole is created.[12] This is the way in which the house was built, taking its place among the other 'visual statements in space' that characterize Rietveld's work. And this is precisely what we tried to emphasize in the restoration.

The space-dividing elements — the first floor itself, the roof and four walls — shape the spatial structure of the house. Within this structure there are five areas of transition from outside to inside, or vice versa. Four of these are horizontal, one on each of the three sides of the house and one at the eastern corner, and one vertical, running through the centre of the house.

The arrangement of space-determining elements in the first transition — between the large undivided wall-surface on Prins Hendriklaan and the adjoining house — begins by the gate onto the street.[13] This continues along a paved pathway, a patio, a balcony, an eave, a pillar with railings and, on the ground floor and upstairs, window-frames and door-frames with a balanced asymmetrical composition. The window-frames are set high in the wall to contribute to the privacy necessary on the street side. The door on the ground floor is a half door like a stable door, and beside this is a small vitrine-like window:[14] here Mrs Schröder exhibited paintings that she had for sale by friends like Bart van der Leck and Bendien. Grey wall surfaces extend from outside inwards to the level of the top of the door.
On the first floor a space *between* outside and inside is created by the balcony and the eaves. The grey surface that continues outside from inside is the beginning (or the end) of a spatial composition that extends via the wall cupboards, wall covering and the beds, the coloured areas on the floor and the white cupboard, into the middle of the house.[15]

In the second area the transition is organized between the space outside and the study, the hall and the boy's room.[16] This begins outside with the gates and paths. In front of the study is another patio. At the junction between exterior and interior there is a seat here, inside and outside. The glass surfaces of the window and the door can be closed off with a kind of wooden shutter. The study[17] is the most contemplative place in the house, with its side wall without a window, the shading or 'hooding' effect of the under side of the balcony, and the relatively large black surfaces of wall and ceiling. In the hallway, the border between inside and outside is delineated by a stable door and a glass protruding cupboard with a small letter box and shelves for toys for use outdoors.[18] All the areas of the house meet in the hall, not only via the doors, but also visually through strips of glass placed just below the ceiling.[19]
In front of the boy's room lies the balcony, which juts into the outside space.[20] When it grew dark, removable wooden shutters were placed in front of the glass surfaces; during the day these wooden shutters had special storage places in the room. A grey shutter for the window hung in the daytime above the washbasin and hid a mirror. A blue shutter for the narrower of the balcony doors hung on one of the sliding partitions, and a black shutter for the wider door, stood at the foot of the bed.[21] Everything in the house contributes to the total effect, even when not actually in use.

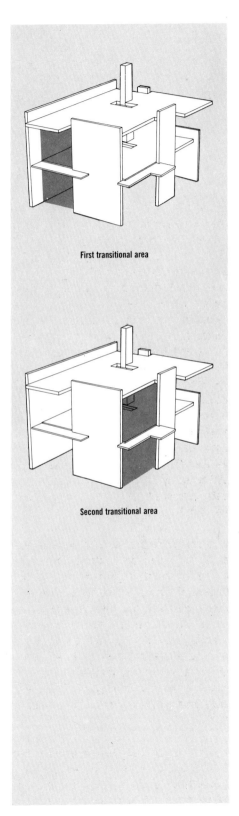

First transitional area

Second transitional area

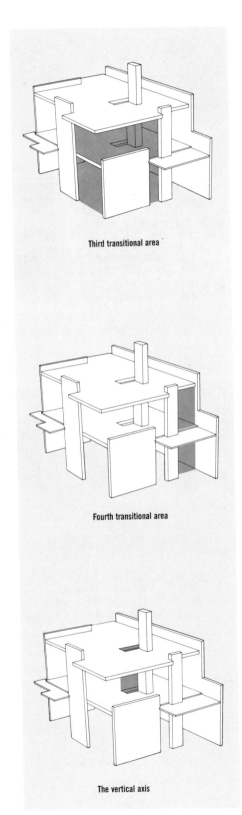

Third transitional area

Fourth transitional area

The vertical axis

The third transitional area lies at the eastern corner of the house, with the kitchen on the ground floor and the living area upstairs.[22] The kitchen window has a high sill, which afforded a measure of seclusion as it originally looked across the wide, open polder. By the window was a system for delivering goods so that Mrs Schröder didn't have to go downstairs to collect them. Outside was a small red pillar on the high sill with the message 'Goods to be delivered here' which functioned as a sign to show tradesmen where to go.[23] A speaking tube in the wall enabled them to talk to someone upstairs. By regulating the system that locked the kitchen window, Mrs Schröder ensured that tradesmen could open it themselves. There was a folding shelf behind that window, on which the deliveries could be placed from outside. At night, the kitchen window was closed with shutters which were laid on top of the cupboard during the day.[24] The glass in the outside door can be closed off and protected with a hinged shutter.[25]
When the windows are open, the living area upstairs functions like a large covered balcony opening onto the polder. Then the distinction between inside and outside disappears completely, particularly as the roof juts out a long way here.[26]

The fourth transitional area contains a patio and a balcony that overlap with the third area, the window and door of the room of the household help and the window of Mrs Schröder's bedroom.[27] The glass surfaces of both the door and the window of the room on the ground floor can be closed off with shutters. The walls and ceiling of this room are yellow, probably because it gets no sunlight.
When the windows in Mrs Schröder's bedroom are open it seems as if the yellow part of the wall extends outside and the bed is standing on the balcony. The cupboard containing the washbasin in this room is the summit of simplicity. It is also striking that the metal expansion tank of the central heating is completely exposed in the bedroom.

The last area in which the transition between inside and outside is determined vertically, lies at the centre of the house. It begins downstairs in the hall with the half-landing and the bench[28] that was used when telephone calls were made and continues with the stairs, the blue chimney column and the skylight with its rectangular, box-like glass roof extension.[29] The stream of light from above can be regulated by means of a trap door which can be fixed in three different positions. In the middle position it is possible to climb up to the trap door with a small ladder that fastens onto the protective stair railings,[30] and from there to climb onto the roof through a little door in the glass roof extension. Mrs Schröder's children used to climb onto the trap door to play up there. The stairwell area can be closed off from the living-dining area with wooden sliding partitions and a movable window.[31]
In all the transitional areas of the house, except in Mrs Schröder's bedroom, the relationship between inside and outside is not only tangibly present, it is also physically possible to move from inside to outside, onto the patios, the balconies and the roof.

When Mrs Schröder died the house was filled with the memories of her life there. These have disappeared with its restoration. No-one lives there now, yet the house is not empty; some other quality fills it. Han Schröder — who with her mother discussed the restoration work with me in 1973 — came to Holland from the USA for the official handing over of the house to the city of Utrecht in 1987, and was faced with the metamorphosis of the home in which she had grown up. Afterwards she wrote to the Rietveld Schröder House Foundation about this experience:

'I think this house has become something spatially beautiful, an object, a work of art in which personal, human memories are not transmitted to the visitor, yet the record of human life is clearly recognisable like some finely-woven tissue. I suspect that my mother would have appreciated this; Rietveld thought that time made visible was something "fascinating and attractive" but I don't think he wanted to be distracted or influenced by it. (...) This house once more clearly reveals the ideas that Rietveld and my mother conceived and developed, shows what they were able to achieve here, and where these ideas had their limitations. This house neither was nor is, as I see it, an architectural monument, a declaration or manifesto; it was an original, new attitude towards life given physical form.'

22. see ill. pp.6-7,105

23. see ill. p.111

24. see ill. p.59

25. see ill. p.62

26. see ill. pp.76,77

27. see ill. p.78

28. see ill. pp.30,58

29. see ill. pp.10,24-25,102,103

30. see ill. p.67

31. see ill. pp.11,67,86-87

# Bibliography

Baljeu, Joost;
*Theo van Doesburg*
New York, Macmillan, 1974

Banham, Reyner;
*Theory and Design in the First Machine Age*
London, The Architectural Press, 1960

Baroni, Daniele;
*I mobili di Gerrit Thomas Rietveld*
Milano, Gruppo Editoriale Electa, 1977
*The furniture of Gerrit Thomas Rietveld*
Woodbury, New York, Barron's, 1978

Bless, Frits;
*Rietveld 1888-1964. Een biografie*
Amsterdam/Baarn, Bert Bakker/Erven Thomas Rap, 1982

Blotkamp, Carel; Mulder, Bertus; Rook, Gerrit Jan de;
*Rietveld Schröder Huis 1925-1975*
Utrecht, A.W. Bruna & Zoon, 1975
2nd edition: *Rietveld Schröder Huis*
Utrecht, Impress bv, 1984

Blotkamp, Carel (et.al.);
*De beginjaren van De Stijl 1917-1922*
Utrecht, Reflex, 1982
*De Stijl: The Formative Years 1917-1922*
Cambridge, Massachusetts/London, The MIT Press, 1983

Brattinga, Pieter (ed.);
*Rietveld, 1924. Schröder Huis*
Hilversum, Kwadraatblad Steendrukkerij De Jong & Co, 1963
reprint: Utrecht, Reflex, 1985 (Dutch-English)

Brown, Theodore M.;
*The work of G. Rietveld Architect*
Utrecht, A.W. Bruna & Zoon, 1958

Brown, Theodore M.;
*Rietveld's Egocentric Vision*
Journal of the Society of Architectural Historians
Dec. 1965, Vol. XXIv, No. 4, p. 292 ff

Dittrich, Katinka; Blom, Paul; Bool, Flip (eds.);
*Berlijn-Amsterdam 1920-1940. Wisselwerkingen*
Amsterdam, Em. Querido's Uitgeverij bv. 1982

Drijver, Peter; Niemeijer, Johannes;
*Werkboek: Rietveld Meubels om zelf te maken/Workbook: How to construct Rietveld Furniture*
Delft, Academia, 1986 (Dutch-English)

Fannelli, Giovanni;
*Moderne Architectuur in Nederland 1900-1940*
Den Haag, Staatsuitgeverij, 1978

Kroon, Ben;
*De geboorte van het Rietveld Schröder Huis*
De Tijd, 29 November 1974

Lissitzky-Küppers, Sophie;
*El Lissitzky. Maler, Architekt, Typograf, Fotograf*
Dresden, Verlag der Kunst, 1967
*El Lissitzky. Life Letters Texts*
London, Thames and Hudson Ltd, 1968
Reprinted with revisions, 1980

Nagtegaal, Corrie;
*Tr. Schröder-Schräder, Bewoonster van het Rietveld Schröderhuis*
Utrecht, Impress bv, 1987

Petersen, Ad (ed.);
*De Stijl* (complete reprint)
Amsterdam, Van Gennep, 1968

Rens, Helma van (ed.);
*Gerrit Rietveld Teksten*
Utrecht, Impress bv, 1979

Rooij, Max van;
*Rietveld Schröder Huis*
De Vorm, Maandblad voor Vormgeving, June-July 1975

Rothuizen, William;
*De maximale eenvoud van Rietveld*
Haagse Post, 24 July 1982

Schippers, K.;
*Holland Dada*
Amsterdam, Em. Querido's Uitgeverij bv, 1974

Smithson, Alison and Peter;
*The Heroic Period of Modern Architecture*
London, Thames and Hudson Ltd, 1981
An earlier version of this Heroic Period was first published in:
Architectural Design, December 1965, Whitefriars Press

Straaten, Evert van;
*Theo van Doesburg 1883-1931*
Den Haag, Staatsuitgeverij, 1983

Troy, Nancy J.;
*The De Stijl Environment*
Cambridge, Massachusetts/London, The MIT Press, 1983

Troy, Nancy J.;
*The totally harmonious interior: paradise or prison?*
Piet Mondrian lecture, Sikkensprijs Foundation, 1985

Exhibition cat.;
*G. Rietveld Architect*
Stedelijk Museum Amsterdam 1971 / Hayward Gallery London 1972

Exhibition cat.;
*Bart van der Leck 1876-1958*
Stedelijk Museum Amsterdam / Rijksmuseum Kröller-Müller Otterlo 1975

Exhibition cat.;
*Nederlandse Architectuur 1856-1934*
*Berlage*
Haags Gemeentemuseum, Den Haag
1975

Exhibition cat.;
*Nederlandse Architectuur 1880-1930*
*Americana*
Rijksmuseum Kröller-Müller, Otterlo
1975

Exhibition cat.;
*De Stijl 1917-1931, Visions of Utopia*
Walker Art Centre Minneapolis /
Hirschhorn Museum Washington 1982
Minneapolis/New York, Abbeville Press
Publishers, 1982
*De Stijl 1917-1931*
Stedelijk Museum Amsterdam / Rijks-
museum Kröller-Müller Otterlo 1982
Amsterdam, Meulenhoff/Landshoff,
1982

Exhibition cat.;
*Het Nieuwe Bouwen: Voorgeschiedenis*
*/ Previous History*
Nederlands Documentatiecentrum voor
de Bouwkunst Amsterdam 1982
Delft/Amsterdam, Delft University Press,
1982 (Dutch-English)

Exhibition cat.;
*Het Nieuwe Bouwen: Rotterdam 1920-*
*1960*
Museum Boymans-van Beuningen
Rotterdam 1982
Delft/Rotterdam, Delft University Press,
1982 (Dutch-English)

Exhibition cat.;
*Het Nieuwe Bouwen: De Stijl,*
*De Nieuwe Beelding in de Architectuur*
*/ Neo Plasticism in Architecture*
Haags Gemeentemuseum Den Haag
1983
Delft/Den Haag, Delft University Press,
1983 (Dutch-English)

Exhibition cat.;
*Het Nieuwe Bouwen: CIAM,*
*Internationaal / International*
*Volkshuisvesting Stedebouw / Housing*
*Town Planning*
Rijksmuseum Kröller-Müller Otterlo 1983
Delft/Otterlo, Delft University Press,
1983 (Dutch-English)

Exhibition cat.;
*Rietveld als meubelmaker, wonen met*
*experimenten 1900-1924*
Centraal Museum Utrecht 1983

Exhibition cat.;
*De Stijl et l'Architecture en France*
Institut Français d'Architecture Paris
1985
Liège/Bruxelles, Pierre Mardaga; éditeur,
1985

Exhibition cat.;
*2D/3D: Art and Craft Made and*
*Designed in the 20th Century*
Laing Art Gallery Newcastle upon Tyne /
Northern Centre for Contemporary Arts
Sunderland 1987

# Index

This book was the idea of Lenneke
Büller and Frank den Oudsten,
and was made possible through the
cooperation of Cees de Jong,
Vorm + Kleur.

*Foreword*
Wim Crouwel

*Text*
Paul Overy
Lenneke Büller, Frank den Oudsten
Bertus Mulder

*Translation*
Wendie Shaffer

*Photographs*
Frank den Oudsten

With the exception of:
E.A. Blitz & Zn., pp.24-25,84
Ad Windig, p. 41
The State Service for Preservation of
Monuments and Historical Buildings,
p. 80
Jan Versnel, pp. 84, 85
Cas Oorthuys p. 85 below
Floor Lem, pp. 110, 112
© Bart van der Leck, Piet Mondrian,
Gerrit Rietveld 1988 c/o Beeldrecht
Amsterdam.

*Graphic design*
Cees de Jong, Ernst Schilp
Vorm + Kleur grafisch ontwerpers

*Editor*
Lenneke Büller

*Archives/Collections*
The drawings, documentary photographic
material, etc., come from the Schröder
Archives, the Rietveld Schröder House
Collection, custody of the Central
Museum, Utrecht

With the exception of:
City Archives Utrecht, pp.24-25,84
Netherlands Office for Fine Arts, The
Hague, archive Theo and Nelly van
Doesburg, gift Van Moorsel, pp. 47, 70,
72 below
Dutch Documentation Centre for
Architecture, Amsterdam, archive Van
Eesteren, p. 71
Federal State Gallery, graphic collec-
tions, Stuttgart, p. 72 above
State Service for Preservation of
Monuments and Historical Buildings,
Zeist, p. 80
Haags Gemeentemuseum, The Hague,
p. 91 below
Private collection, p. 94

Wayne

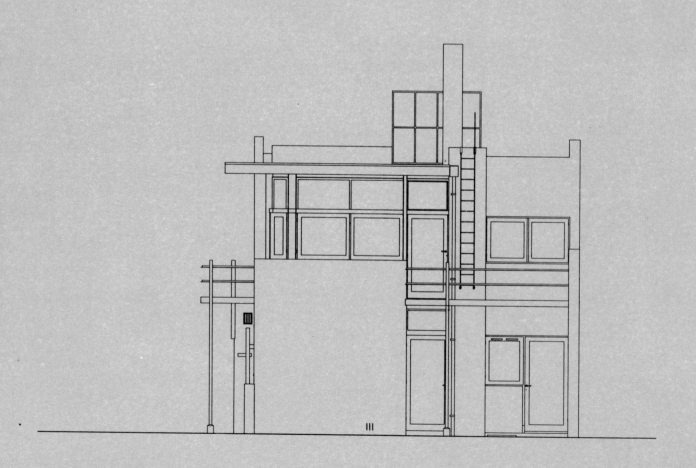